Never Be Sick Again Official Workbook

ACCESS SUPERNATURAL HEALTH THROUGH JESUS' RESURRECTION POWER

CHAD GONZALES

Copyright 2024–Harrison House

All rights reserved. This book is protected by the copyright laws of the United States of America. This book may not be copied or reprinted for commercial gain or profit. The use of short quotations or occasional page copying for personal or group study is permitted and encouraged. Permission will be granted upon request. Unless otherwise indicated, all scripture quotations are taken from the *King James Version* of the Bible. Used by permission. All rights reserved.

All emphasis within Scripture quotations is the author's own. Please note that Harrison House's publishing style capitalizes certain pronouns in Scripture that refer to the Father, Son, and Holy Spirit, and may differ from some publishers' styles. Take note that the name satan and related names are not capitalized. We choose not to acknowledge him, even to the point of violating grammatical rules.

Harrison House P.O. Box 310, Shippensburg, PA 17257-0310

This book and all other Harrison House's books are available at Christian bookstores and distributors worldwide.

For Worldwide Distribution.

Reach us on the Internet: www.harrisonhouse.com.

ISBN 13 TP: 978-1-6675-1002-6

ISBN 13 eBook: 978-1-6675-1003-3

CONTENTS

Introduction	v
1. In The Garden	1
2. Delivered From Egypt	8
3. Healing Under The Old Covenant	14
4. A Better Covenant	20
5. THE COVENANT OF GRACe	26
6. The True Gospel Of Healing	32
7. THE REAL MEANING OF 1 PETER 2:24	39
8. The Day You Became Alive	45
9. Made Perfect	52
10. Filled with Life	59
11. The Flow in You	66
12. Who Do You Think You Are?	72
13. Receiving Your Healing Is for the Sinner	78
14. You Are the Body of Christ	84
15. Don't Get Cheated	92
16. Our Belief in Sickness	98
17. A New Kingdom	104
18. Substituting Brass For Gold	110
19. Generational Curses and Your Bloodline	116
20. SATAN ISN'T TRESPASSING ON YOUR BODY	123
21. Whatever Has Your Imagination Has Your Faith	131
22. Stay Connected to the Source	139
23. When Christians Are Sick	146
24. Accidents and Injuries	153
25. Food And Drugs	160
About the Publisher	167

INTRODUCTION

Welcome to the "Never Be Sick Again Official Workbook," a comprehensive guide designed to empower you with the knowledge and tools to lead a healthier, more fulfilling life. This workbook accompanies the transformative book "Never Be Sick Again," expanding upon its teachings and providing practical applications to help you integrate these principles into your daily life.

As you embark on this journey through the workbook, you'll dive deep into a variety of topics that challenge conventional understandings of health, disease, and healing. Our goal is to shift your perspective from merely treating symptoms to fostering an environment within your body that promotes overall wellness and prevents illness.

UNDERSTANDING THE FOUNDATIONS

The foundational belief of "Never Be Sick Again" is that health is a choice. This workbook builds on that premise by exploring how

INTRODUCTION

every decision you make—what you eat, how you manage stress, and your physical activity—directly impacts your health. You'll discover that you are not merely a bystander in your health journey but an active participant capable of changing the outcome of your life.

KEY TAKEAWAYS

- **Your Body, God's Temple**: Learn to see your body as the temple of the Holy Spirit. This recognition will transform your approach to what you consume and how you treat your physical form.
- **Holistic Health Perspective**: Gain insights into how spiritual, mental, and physical health are interconnected and how imbalances in one area can affect the others.
- **Diet and Nutrition:** Delve into the roles of different foods and their impacts on your body. Understand the detrimental effects of processed foods and the benefits of whole, unprocessed foods.
- **Exercise as a Pillar of Health**: Explore the critical role of physical activity in maintaining health and preventing diseases.
- **The Power of the Mind**: Learn about the significant influence your thoughts and emotions have on your physical health. Understand the connection between stress management and wellness.
- **Spiritual Health**: Deepen your spiritual practices and understand how spiritual well-being can manifest in physical health.
- **Environmental Factors**: Assess how your

INTRODUCTION

environment affects your health—from the products you use at home to your broader living conditions.
- **Preventive Health Practices**: Focus on prevention as a primary approach, reducing the need for medical interventions by maintaining a healthy lifestyle.
- **Empowerment Through Education**: Become equipped with the knowledge to make informed health decisions that align with God's design for a healthy life.
- **Community and Support**: Recognize the importance of community in supporting your health journey, including the role of accountability and encouragement from others.

WHAT YOU WILL RECEIVE FROM THIS WORKBOOK

- **Interactive Exercises**: Engage with practical activities designed to apply the concepts discussed in each chapter, helping to reinforce learning and encourage real-world application.
- **Reflective Questions**: Each chapter includes reflective questions that prompt you to think critically about how the information presented affects you personally and how you can implement changes.
- **Action Steps**: Clear, actionable steps are provided to help you translate knowledge into action. These include simple lifestyle adjustments and larger, goal-oriented plans.
- **Personal Assessments**: Tools to help you evaluate your current health status and track your progress as you implement new strategies.

INTRODUCTION

- **Scriptural Insights**: Each section is grounded in biblical principles, offering spiritual encouragement and scriptural references to reinforce the messages of stewardship over your health.

By the end of this workbook, you will not only have a deeper understanding of the principles laid out in "Never Be Sick Again" but also practical tools and strategies to transform these principles into a sustainable, healthy lifestyle. This journey is about taking control of your health, empowering yourself with knowledge, and living in accordance with God's perfect design for your life.

Prepare to embark on a transformative journey that challenges conventional wisdom, arms you with essential knowledge, and aligns your physical practices with your spiritual beliefs. Welcome to a life where being sick again is no longer an inevitable part of your story.

CHAPTER 1
IN THE GARDEN

God's original design for humanity was one of wholeness, health, and divine connection. Even in the face of sin's consequences, His mercy provided protection and a plan for redemption. Remember that in Christ, we have access to the life that was lost, and we are called to live in a way that reflects His nature.

"Beloved, I pray that you may prosper in all things and be in health, just as your soul prospers." - 3 John 1:2 (NKJV)

In the profound narrative of Genesis, the story of creation unfolds with a beautiful, deliberate sequence, showing us how life was designed to flourish. From the outset, the **Order of Creation Reflects Life's Self-Sustaining Design.** On the third day, the earth sprouts vegetation, each species endowed with the capacity to reproduce according to its own kind. This pattern of life—be it an oak tree producing acorns that grow into new oaks, or apple trees flourishing from the seeds of their fruit—demonstrates a divine blueprint where each element of creation supports the cycle of life, nurturing and sustaining future generations.

By the fifth and sixth days, the creation story expands to include all creatures of the sea, the birds of the air, and all land animals. Each creature, from the smallest fish to the greatest whale, is infused with life and the inherent ability to multiply, ensuring the perpetuation of their species. Amid this burgeoning life, a unique act of creation occurs: **Mankind Is Uniquely Created in God's Image.** Unlike other creatures, humans are fashioned not only to bear God's image but to steward the vast creation before them. This distinction is profound, emphasizing that humans are created with a higher purpose, not just to inhabit the earth but to oversee it, reflecting God's wisdom and care.

This unique position carries an extraordinary responsibility and privilege. **Man as the "God-kind" Possesses Divine Likeness and Authority**, tasked with the stewardship of the earth. This is not a dominion born of tyranny but a guardianship that mirrors God's own rule—benevolent, wise, and nurturing. It's clear then that humans are meant to reflect God's character in their rule, stewarding creation with justice and mercy, guiding the natural world towards flourishing and balance.

The Breath of Life: Humanity's Divine DNA marks a pivotal moment in creation. When God breathes life into Adam, it's not mere respiration but the infusion of a spiritual and life-giving essence. This act distinguishes humans from all other forms of life. This breath, this spirit, is nothing less than the impartation of God's own nature into humankind, a gift that carries profound implications for our understanding of human dignity and destiny.

Originally, **God's Original Design Excluded Sickness and**

Death. The world as it was made was perfect in its harmony, untouched by disease or decay. In this flawless creation, everything was imbued with life, and that life was meant to sustain itself in perpetuity without the interference of death or disease. This truth underscores a significant theological point: sickness and death are not creations of God but aberrations that entered through sin.

Indeed, **Sin as the Root of Sickness and Mortality** introduced disruption into this perfect order. When Adam and Eve chose to disobey God, the spiritual death they incurred severed their—and by extension, humanity's—direct communion with God. This spiritual rupture had physical manifestations: the body, once immortal and perfect, became mortal and flawed, subject to the ravages of age, illness, and decay.

However, even in judgment, God's compassion is evident. **God's Merciful Provision of the Immune System** as a complex defense mechanism within the human body underscores His grace. Knowing that sin would mar creation, God designed the immune system to protect us from the myriad pathogens that could harm us, a testament to His foreknowledge and His continued care for creation, even in a fallen state.

The tragic necessity of **Expulsion from the Garden as a Merciful Act** reveals another layer of God's mercy. By expelling Adam and Eve from Eden and barring access to the Tree of Life, God prevented humanity from an eternal, unending existence in a state of fallenness and separation from Him. This act, though punitive, was also protective, preserving the possibility of redemption.

The Continuous Flow of Death Affects All of Humanity, underscoring the pervasive impact of Adam's sin. This hereditary spiritual death passes to all people, manifesting as physical decay and moral corruption, which only the redemptive work of Christ can reverse.

IN THE GARDEN

Finally, the narrative of Genesis, and the promise within it, points to **The Promise of Redemption and Restoration of Life**. The seeds of the gospel are sown early in Scripture, as God promises that the seed of the woman would crush the serpent's head. This prophetic declaration points forward to Jesus Christ, who through His death and resurrection, would restore not only spiritual life to fallen humanity but also promises a future where death, mourning, and pain will be no more.

REFLECTIVE QUESTIONS

1. How does understanding God's original design for health and life influence your view on sickness today?
2. In what ways does knowing that humanity is made in God's image affect how you perceive your identity and purpose?
3. How does the concept of an "immune system as a backup plan" impact your view of God's mercy and foresight?
4. How do you think Adam's sin and its effects on humanity shape our understanding of the necessity of salvation?
5. How can you apply the lesson of divine likeness and intended dominion in your own life and daily choices?

ACTIONABLE STEPS

- **Cultivate**: Cultivate a deeper sense of gratitude for God's design and mercy. Reflect on the marvel of the

immune system and God's foresight, acknowledging that even the human body's resilience is a gift from a loving Creator.
- **Equip**: Equip yourself with knowledge of your identity in God's image. Study the scriptural passages that emphasize humanity's unique creation and purpose, focusing on Genesis 1 and 2, and meditate on the implications of being made in God's likeness.
- **Engage**: Engage in mindful living that aligns with God's intentions. Make choices that reflect stewardship of your body and surroundings, knowing that you were created to live, walk, and operate like God on earth, with purpose and integrity.

Journaling Prompt

Reflect on what it means to be made in the image of God. How does this truth affect your daily life, health decisions, and relationships? Write about how understanding God's original design changes your perspective on wholeness and purpose.

IN THE GARDEN

NEVER BE SICK AGAIN OFFICIAL WORKBOOK

CHAPTER 2
DELIVERED FROM EGYPT

God's plan always provides for our deliverance and healing. Just as He liberated the Israelites from Egypt with mighty signs and wonders, He offers us freedom from the bondage of sin and sickness through Jesus Christ. Trust in His provision and power to lead you into a life of health and spiritual abundance.

"He also brought them out with silver and gold, and there was none feeble among His tribes." - Psalm 105:37 (NKJV)

From the onset of **DELIVERED FROM EGYPT**, we delve into a remarkable period in biblical history that underscores the profoundness of God's deliverance. The **miracle night of the Passover** is a testament to God's power not only to save but to heal. On this night, as detailed in Exodus 12, the Israelites experienced perhaps the largest mass healing ever recorded. From the youngest to the oldest, every individual among the estimated one to two million Hebrews was touched by God's healing power. This event wasn't just a display of divine might; it was a preparation for their journey from bondage to freedom, ensuring they were physically capable of undertaking the trek to the Promised Land.

As we reflect on the **significant healing during Passover**, it's clear that God's interventions are both purposeful and holistic. By healing His people physically, God was preparing them not just for immediate freedom but for the covenantal relationship He desired to establish with them—a relationship marked by His continual provision and care. This healing was a clear demonstration that God cared for their every need, underscoring that **none were feeble** as they exited Egypt, a fulfillment of Psalm 105:37.

This profound healing event serves as a **type and shadow of the ultimate healing** available through Jesus Christ, our Passover Lamb. Just as the Israelites applied the blood of the lamb to their doorposts and were spared from death, so too are we spared from eternal death by the blood of Christ. This parallel extends to the physical healings they experienced; in Christ, we find healing from sin and the effects of the fall, including sickness and death.

The covenant of healing established at Marah, as recounted in Exodus 15, further cements the idea that God desires not just spiritual but physical well-being for His people. Here, God promises that if the Israelites heed His commandments, they will not suffer the diseases that plagued the Egyptians. This promise not only highlights God's role as healer but also sets a precedent for the blessings of obedience.

As we consider the breadth of God's miracles—from the **healings in Goshen** to the **spectacular deliverance at the Red Sea**—it becomes evident that God's deliverance is comprehensive. It encompasses freedom from physical ailments, liberation from spiritual bondage, and provision for every need. Each act of deliverance, each provision, and each healing during the Exodus was a step toward fulfilling God's promises to Abraham and a foreshadowing of the greater deliverance to come through Christ.

REFLECTIVE QUESTIONS

1. What does the healing during the Passover reveal about God's priorities for His people?
2. How does the concept of Jesus as our Passover Lamb influence your understanding of His sacrificial death and resurrection?
3. In what ways does the promise at Marah deepen your appreciation for the connection between obedience and divine blessing?
4. How can the examples of God's deliverance in Exodus inspire confidence in His ability to provide for your needs today?
5. Reflect on a time when you experienced God's healing or deliverance. How did that experience impact your faith?

ACTIONABLE STEPS

- **Cultivate**: Develop a deeper appreciation for God's historical acts of deliverance and healing. Reflect on the Passover and its significance both historically and spiritually as a demonstration of God's power and mercy.

- **Equip**: Study the deeper theological implications of the Exodus story. Explore how the themes of liberation and covenant are woven throughout the Bible, culminating in the work of Christ.
- **Engage**: Apply the principles of trust and obedience seen in the Exodus to your own life. Consider areas where you need to trust God more fully and commit to following Him more closely, especially in difficult or uncertain times.

Journaling Prompt

Reflect on the relationship between God's acts of deliverance and His desire for a covenant relationship with His people. How does understanding this relationship affect your view of God's character and His plans for your life? Write about how you can live in a way that reflects a deep trust in God's deliverance and provision.

DELIVERED FROM EGYPT

NEVER BE SICK AGAIN OFFICIAL WORKBOOK

CHAPTER 3
HEALING UNDER THE OLD COVENANT

In the strength and promise of God, we find not only our deliverance but also our healing. Just as He vowed to keep the Israelites free from the diseases known in Egypt, so too does He promise to protect us from the ailments of sin through our faith in Jesus Christ. Embrace His promises and live under the canopy of His faithful commitment to our well-being.

"And the Lord will take away from you all sickness, and will afflict you with none of the terrible diseases of Egypt which you have known, but will lay them on all those who hate you." - Deuteronomy 7:15 (NKJV)

HEALING UNDER THE OLD COVENANT, we explore the profound depths of God's promises to the Israelites as outlined in Deuteronomy 7. This scripture vividly illustrates the **conditional promises of health** based on obedience to God's covenant. The Lord's assurance that no one among the Israelites would be barren and that He would shield them from all sickness powerfully underscores the health and prosperity intended for those who follow His commandments.

The **covenantal relationship** established through Moses brought not only a societal law but also personal blessings that directly impacted the physical well-being of the people. This covenant, which demanded adherence to God's statutes, offered a life free from the diseases that plagued their Egyptian captors. It provided a stark contrast to the life of bondage and illness they had known, highlighting the redemptive power of God's grace when coupled with human obedience.

In these ancient texts, we see a recurring theme: **obedience is intricately linked to health.** The blessings listed in Deuteronomy 7 were not merely spiritual or material but included significant physical aspects—protection from disease, fertility, and overall health. These promises illustrate a foundational truth that God's desire for His people encompasses every facet of human experience.

The historical narrative of the Israelites serves as a **prototype for spiritual truths applicable today.** Their journey from slavery to freedom mirrors our spiritual journey through Christ. Just as the Israelites were called to obey God's laws to receive physical blessings, we are called to follow Christ's teachings to receive not only eternal life but also the fullness of life here and now, which includes health and peace.

The profound implications of the Old Covenant provide a precursor to the superior promises found in the New Covenant through Jesus Christ. While the Old Covenant required strict obedience to avoid curses and gain blessings, the New Covenant offers grace that covers our shortcomings and provides access to God's promises through faith.

HEALING UNDER THE OLD COVENANT

REFLECTIVE QUESTIONS

1. How does the Old Covenant's emphasis on obedience inform your understanding of God's expectations in the New Covenant?
2. What does the promise of health and prosperity under the Old Covenant reveal about God's character and His desires for His people?
3. In what ways does the physical healing in the Old Covenant point to the spiritual healing offered through Jesus?
4. How can the lessons from the Israelites' experience enhance your daily walk of faith?
5. What steps can you take to align more closely with God's commands and access the blessings He has promised?

ACTIONABLE STEPS

- **Cultivate**: Strengthen your understanding of the covenantal promises by studying the conditions under which God offered health and protection in the Old Testament.
- **Equip**: Equip yourself with the knowledge of how these Old Covenant principles are fulfilled and expanded in Christ. Reflect on the scriptures that promise healing and protection in the New Testament.
- **Engage**: Actively seek to live out the principles of obedience and faithfulness in your daily life, trusting

that God's promises of health and protection are as relevant today as they were to the Israelites.

JOURNALING **Prompt**

Consider the relationship between obedience and health as illustrated in Deuteronomy 7. Reflect on areas in your life where obedience to God's word could enhance your spiritual and physical well-being. Write about the steps you can take to align more fully with God's statutes and the blessings that might follow.

HEALING UNDER THE OLD COVENANT

NEVER BE SICK AGAIN OFFICIAL WORKBOOK

CHAPTER 4
A BETTER COVENANT

We stand under a new promise, one that outshines the old because it was sealed by the life, death, and resurrection of Jesus Christ. In Him, the fullness of God's promises, including healing and health, are yes and amen. Embrace this better covenant, which not only assures us of eternal life but a quality of life that surpasses even the blessings seen under the old covenant.

"But now He has obtained a more excellent ministry, inasmuch as He is also Mediator of a better covenant, which was established on better promises." - Hebrews 8:6 (NKJV)

A **BETTER COVENANT** delves into the transformative power of the New Covenant under Jesus Christ, which surpasses the Old Covenant in its scope and promise. This chapter underscores the **superiority of the New Covenant**, which is not only a continuation of God's grace but an enhancement and fulfillment of the promises once confined to the laws of Moses and the prophets.

The old covenant, detailed in the scriptures, provided God's people with assurances of health, prosperity, and protection contingent upon their strict obedience. Yet, these blessings, as profound as they were, are dwarfed by the **new promises found in Christ**. Under the New Covenant, these promises are not only expanded but are also made more accessible through faith rather than strict adherence to law.

This chapter invites believers to consider why, despite having a better covenant, many do not experience its full benefits. The problem often lies not with the covenant itself but with our understanding and reception of it. Much like the distortions in a game of telephone, **misunderstandings and miscommunications** have often diluted the purity of the gospel handed down from Christ through the apostles.

Hebrews 8:6 does not merely suggest a slight improvement but declares a profound enhancement of our spiritual heritage. This covenant brings not only reconciliation with God but also a restoration of all things, including our health and well-being. It's an invitation to live fully in the freedom Christ has secured, a life marked not by occasional spiritual highs but by a sustained victory over sin and sickness.

Reflecting on this chapter compels us to revisit and **realign our understanding with the Bible's original message of healing**. It challenges us to shed any layers of religious tradition or personal skepticism that may cloud the pure gospel of Christ. By returning to the source—Jesus and His word—we ensure that our understanding remains untainted by human interpretation or cultural adaptation.

In exploring the implications of this better covenant, we are called to recognize that **Jesus is not only our Savior but also**

our Healer—a role that He fulfilled during His ministry on Earth and continues to fulfill in the lives of believers today.

Reflective Questions

1. How does the New Covenant under Jesus Christ enhance the promises made under the Old Covenant?
2. Why is it important to directly engage with the scriptures when understanding the promises of healing and health?
3. How can misconceptions about healing under the New Covenant affect our experience of God's promises?
4. In what ways can we better align our lives with the teachings of Jesus to fully experience the benefits of the better covenant?
5. What role does faith play in activating the promises of the New Covenant in our lives?

Actionable Steps

- **Cultivate:** Develop a daily habit of studying the scriptures related to the New Covenant, focusing on the comprehensive work of Jesus Christ.
- **Equip:** Equip yourself with historical and theological understanding of how the New Covenant was perceived and taught by the early church.
- **Engage:** Commit to a lifestyle that reflects your faith in the New Covenant's promises—actively trust in

God's provision for health and well-being as integral to your faith walk.

JOURNALING Prompt

Reflect on the "better promises" of the New Covenant as mentioned in Hebrews 8:6. Consider areas in your life where you may have settled for less than what God has promised. Write about how you can shift your mindset and actions to fully embrace and experience these better promises in your everyday life.

A BETTER COVENANT

NEVER BE SICK AGAIN OFFICIAL WORKBOOK

CHAPTER 5
THE COVENANT OF GRACE

Our exploration into the profound depths of God's grace reveals a covenant that is not based on our merits but solely on His promises. It is a covenant of grace, under which we stand not because of our works but through faith in the completed work of Christ.

"For I received from the Lord that which I also delivered to you: that the Lord Jesus on the same night in which He was betrayed took bread; and when He had given thanks, He broke it and said, 'Take, eat; this is My body which is broken for you; do this in remembrance of Me.' In the same manner He also took the cup after supper, saying, 'This cup is the new covenant in My blood. This do, as often as you drink it, in remembrance of Me.' For as often as you eat this bread and drink this cup, you proclaim the Lord's death till He comes."
- 1 Corinthians 11:23-26 (NKJV)

THE COVENANT OF GRACE unfolds the remarkable story of God's deliverance of the Israelites from Egypt—a precursor to the salvation brought through Jesus Christ. This chapter delves deeply into the **significance of the Passover** and its correlation to the covenant established through Christ, highlighting how the events of Exodus were a shadow of the greater redemption to come.

The grace revealed through the old covenant, especially through God's promises to Abraham, was always pointing towards the establishment of a **new and better covenant**. This new covenant, unlike the old, does not depend on human efforts but is rooted in divine grace, making the benefits of the covenant accessible through faith rather than adherence to law.

This chapter discusses how, under the old covenant, blessings were conditional, heavily reliant on strict obedience. In contrast, the new covenant introduces a paradigm where blessings are a result of God's grace through faith in Christ. It's not just an improvement but a transformation of the covenant relationship between God and man.

The new covenant is characterized by better promises because it is mediated by Christ, who not only fulfills the law but enhances every promise through His grace. This includes healing, which, under the new covenant, becomes a testament to God's will for our wholeness and health, reflecting the full extent of His grace.

Reflecting on the new covenant leads to a reevaluation of our understanding of healing and divine health. Unlike the old covenant, which required the Israelites' compliance to receive health, the new covenant secures our health through Christ's atonement, emphasizing that **healing is a part of the atonement**.

THE COVENANT OF GRACE

REFLECTIVE QUESTIONS

1. How does the new covenant of grace differ fundamentally from the old covenant in terms of conditions for healing?
2. What role does faith play in accessing the promises of the new covenant, including healing?
3. How can understanding the covenant of grace change our approach to prayer and receiving from God?
4. Reflect on a time when you experienced God's grace in your life. How did it shape your understanding of His promises?
5. How can the church better teach and embody the truths of the new covenant to empower believers today?

ACTIONABLE STEPS

- **Cultivate:** Build a daily practice of meditating on the promises of the new covenant, particularly those that affirm our health and redemption.
- **Equip:** Educate yourself and others about the theological shifts from the old to the new covenant, emphasizing how these changes impact our daily lives.
- **Engage:** Actively share your understanding of the new covenant with others, offering prayers of faith for healing and demonstrating the grace of God in your community.

JOURNALING Prompt

Consider the implications of the new covenant in your personal life, especially its promise of health and wholeness. Journal about how this understanding can transform your approach to challenges, particularly in areas where you need healing or restoration. Reflect on how you can apply this grace-filled perspective to support others in your life.

THE COVENANT OF GRACE

NEVER BE SICK AGAIN OFFICIAL WORKBOOK

CHAPTER 6
THE TRUE GOSPEL OF HEALING

Stand firm in the knowledge that through Jesus, you have been granted a life free from the bonds of illness and sin. Embrace this profound truth and walk in the wholeness that His sacrifice has secured for you.

For the law of the Spirit of life in Christ Jesus has made me free from the law of sin and death. Romans 8:2

As we venture deeper into understanding our inheritance under the new covenant through Jesus Christ, let's appreciate the better covenant with better promises that we've been granted. This covenant not only mirrors the old covenant's assurances but magnificently transcends them, providing us not just with life but with a life abundant and free from the ailments that once might have ensnared us. Under the old covenant, adherence to God's commands was essential for health and longevity. But now, through Christ, these promises are not just maintained; they are immensely enhanced.

Reflecting on the scope of human history, it's evident that from Adam until Moses, an unstoppable flow of death plagued humanity—a testament to our inherited disconnection due to Adam's sin. However, this **sin and death connection** wasn't merely a consequence of individual sins but a hereditary spiritual malady affecting all. This foundational flaw was the electrical cord that, unless plugged into the source—sin—meant inevitable death and disease.

When God established His covenant with the Israelites through Moses, it signified a profound shift. It included comprehensive **healing**, which acted like a circuit breaker in an electrical system. As long as the Israelites adhered to God's statutes, this spiritual breaker would cut off the flow of sickness. They were essentially still connected to the socket of sin's power, but conditional obedience kept the deadly current at bay.

The introduction of **grace over law** through Jesus marks a revolutionary transformation in our spiritual lineage. Grace isn't conditional; it doesn't ebb based on our missteps or flow on account of our righteousness. Instead, it's a constant, unending stream of life, making the old conditional promises seem constrained by comparison. Through grace, we're afforded not just temporary reprieves from sickness but a permanent severance from the sources of spiritual and physical decay.

The **Righteousness and Life Connection** under the new covenant ensures that as believers, our health is intrinsically tied to our righteous standing in Christ. This radical realignment means that just as sin once guaranteed death, now righteousness ensures life. This shift from the conditional to the inherent underscores the transformative power of Jesus' sacrifice, which doesn't just cover our sins but annihilates their power over us.

The fundamental change Jesus brought about—**changed connection**—means we're no longer tethered to the life-sapping power of sin. Instead, we're connected to the life-giving power of grace. This new connection doesn't just protect us from sickness; it removes us from under sickness's shadow entirely.

In this new covenant, the notion that the **righteous need not seek healing** because they are inherently positioned in health reshapes our understanding of divine promises. Under the old regime, sickness was a constant threat, kept at bay by adherence to the law. Now, under the new covenant, our inherent health is a testament to our restored relationship with God through Christ.

Integration of Healing and Salvation further underscores that our spiritual wholeness includes physical health. This integration assures us that healing isn't an isolated blessing but a fundamental component of our salvation experience, woven into the very fabric of our relationship with Christ.

The **Scriptural Assurance of Healing** provided by texts such as Isaiah 53:5 and 1 Peter 2:24 affirms that our healing is both a completed act through Christ's atonement and an ongoing state of being. This perspective shifts our focus from seeking healing to recognizing and living out the reality of the healing already accomplished on our behalf.

In living out the reality of our new identity, it becomes clear that we're called not just to accept but to actively **live the reality of healing**. This active living doesn't involve striving to achieve health but rather living from a position of health, assured and secured by our covenant relationship with God through Jesus Christ.

In this light, every aspect of our lives should reflect the truth that we've been given a better promise—a life free from the old covenant's shadows and rich in the realities of God's kingdom. As we embrace this truth, let it permeate every aspect of our existence, empowering us to live fully in the freedom and vitality that is our inheritance in Christ.

Reflective Questions

1. How does understanding the **better covenant with better promises** change your perspective on God's provisions for your life?
2. In what ways does the concept of a **sin and death connection** help explain the human condition before Christ's intervention?
3. How does the transition from **grace over law** influence your daily walk with God?
4. Can you identify how the **Righteousness and Life Connection** manifests in your own life experiences?
5. How do you personally integrate the idea of **healing as a component of salvation** in your faith journey?

Actionable Steps

- **Cultivate** an awareness of your new identity in Christ by meditating on scriptures that emphasize righteousness and life.
- **Equip** yourself with knowledge about the true implications of the new covenant by studying the contrasts between the old and new covenants.
- **Engage** in community discussions or small group studies that explore the practical applications of living out the new covenant promises in everyday life.

JOURNALING Prompt

Reflect on a time when you experienced the reality of God's promises manifesting in your life. How did that moment shape your understanding of God's covenant with you and your expectations for divine health and wholeness?

NEVER BE SICK AGAIN OFFICIAL WORKBOOK

THE TRUE GOSPEL OF HEALING

CHAPTER 7
THE REAL MEANING OF 1 PETER 2:24

You are not just shielded from sickness; you are transformed into a being where sickness cannot find harbor. Remember, Christ's stripes have liberated you from the root of all affliction.

Who Himself bore our sins in His own body on the tree, that we, having died to sins, might live for righteousness—by whose stripes you were healed.

In exploring the depths of 1 Peter 2:24, we come to understand that our healing through Christ is not just an external remedy applied as needed; it is a profound internal transformation. **Jesus bore our sins**, addressing the very root of our separation from God, which included the entry of every sickness and disease into human experience. Through His sacrifice, He not only confronted our sins but also liberated us from the resultant curses, including sickness.

By dying with Christ, we have been **freed from the bondage**

of sickness. This is not a mere pause in the onslaught of illness while we maintain moral rigor; it is a complete cessation from the life where sickness has any claim. Just as Christ rose, leaving behind the grave's hold, we too rise in a new health, untouchable by the decay of this world.

Living in righteousness, which was bestowed upon us through Jesus' sacrifice, places us in a **new realm of existence** where the laws of sin and death no longer apply. Here, healing is not an intermittent miracle but a constant state. This truth should reshape our identity, helping us see ourselves as God sees us—permanently whole.

The phrase **"by His stripes you were healed"** is often recited in times of physical distress, yet its true significance lies deeper. It is a testament to a completed work, where healing became our inheritance the moment righteousness was imputed to us through faith in Christ. This healing is comprehensive, encompassing every aspect of our being because it springs from our new nature in Christ, not from our adherence to law.

Often, we perceive healing as a response to sickness. However, in the new covenant, healing is a state of being that preempts sickness. This **proactive health** is not a reactive shield hastily summoned in the face of disease; it is the very atmosphere of our lives in Christ.

Understanding this shifts our focus from seeking healing to recognizing and walking in the **wholeness** already provided. Our covenant with God through Jesus means that just as sickness found no place in Christ, it finds no place in us. We live not on the defensive, hoping to ward off the next health challenge, but confidently, knowing that the battle against sickness was conclusively won at the cross.

The realignment from old covenant thinking, which sees God as a responder to our infirmities, to new covenant realization, which knows Him as the **preventer of all ailments**, is crucial. It moves us from seeing God merely as a healer to recognizing Him as our health.

This new understanding calls us to **live from health**, not for healing. In the kingdom of God, we operate from a position of victory in every area of our lives, including our health. This is not a promise waiting to be fulfilled; it is a present reality—the life of God in us, which is disease-free and abundant.

To fully grasp and live out this truth, we must **embrace our identity** as the healed, the whole, and the righteous in Christ. This identity doesn't fluctuate with physical symptoms or medical reports; it is as constant and unchanging as the God who declared it over us.

In essence, **1 Peter 2:24** invites us to live in the accomplished reality of our healing, a gift as complete and enduring as our salvation. It is not something we fight to achieve but a fact we stand in, enjoy, and extend to others as the undeniable evidence of God's kingdom at work today.

Reflective Questions

1. What does understanding Jesus bore our sins reveal about the scope of our healing?
2. How does the reality of being freed from the bondage of sickness change your approach to health?
3. In what ways does living in righteousness alter your experience of everyday life?
4. Why is it significant to recognize that by His stripes, you were healed as a completed work?
5. How can embracing your identity as permanently whole influence your mental and spiritual wellbeing?

Actionable Steps

- **Cultivate** a daily practice of declaring your health and wholeness in Christ, reinforcing your new identity.
- **Equip** yourself with biblical truths about your righteous standing and its implications for your health.
- **Engage** in teaching others about the full meaning of healing in the new covenant, helping them to walk in the same revelation and freedom.

Journaling Prompt

Reflect on moments when you've experienced divine health or witnessed healing. How do these experiences align with your understanding of being completely unplugged from the source of sickness, and how can they encourage you to live fully in the reality of your new covenant identity?

THE REAL MEANING OF 1 PETER 2:24

CHAPTER 8
THE DAY YOU BECAME ALIVE

Embrace the new life and identity you have in Christ. You are no longer defined by your past but by God's love and the righteousness of Christ. Stand firm in this truth and let it guide you every day.

"Therefore, if anyone is in Christ, he is a new creation; old things have passed away; behold, all things have become new." - 2 Corinthians 5:17 NKJV

In this chapter titled "The Day You Became Alive," we explore the remarkable transformation that occurs when one enters into a relationship with Christ. As the author, I want to convey to you, the reader, that when you accept Christ, a fundamental change happens, one that the Bible describes using the profound imagery of becoming a new creation. The scripture in **2 Corinthians 5:17** states that if anyone is in Christ, he is a new creation; old things have passed away; behold, all things have become new. This isn't merely poetic language; it signifies a real, tangible change in our spiritual identity.

When discussing the term new, as used in this scripture, we learn that it derives from the Greek word 'kainos,' which implies something freshly made and superior in nature. The concept of **Kainos** highlights that this newness isn't just about being recent but is also an upgrade of our previous selves. This teaches us that becoming a new creation in Christ involves an enhancement, a superior form of ourselves that reflects the heavenly rather than the earthly.

The idea of being born again is often misunderstood. It isn't just a symbolic rebirth but a literal, spiritual one. When Jesus discussed this with Nicodemus in John 3:3, He wasn't proposing a metaphor but a reality where one becomes completely new, akin to a spiritual renaissance. Being **Born Again** means we transition from our old selves into something that never existed before—a being that is born of God, which carries attributes of our heavenly Father, not just our earthly nature.

One of the most intriguing aspects of this transformation is that it may not be visible externally. You might not notice any physical changes, but internally, a seismic shift occurs. This **Invisible Transformation** is significant because it marks the transition of your spirit into a new realm of existence that is aligned with God's kingdom rather than the fallen world.

The scripture from **Romans 6:4** brings us into the profound realization that we identify not just with Christ's death but also with His resurrection. This verse insists that just as Christ was raised from the dead through the glory of the Father, we too should walk in newness of life. This doesn't merely suggest a return to life but an invitation to a quality of life that is divine in its essence.

Furthermore, our relationship with sin and its consequence, which includes sickness, is completely transformed. The Bible makes it clear that in Christ, we are no longer subject to the power of sin or its physical manifestations like sickness. Through Christ's resurrection, we have been made free, suggesting that **Sin and Sickness Overcome** is not just a possibility but our new reality.

This leads us to the breathtaking reality of our **Eternal Connection to God**. Being in Christ means we are now part of an unbreakable bond with the divine. This connection isn't temporary or conditional; it's an eternal state that changes everything from how we live our lives to how we perceive our future.

As we delve deeper into the implications of our new identity, we find that our true life is no longer visible for the world to scrutinize but is **Hidden in Christ with God** as mentioned in Colossians 3:3. This hidden life is safeguarded in the divine, which means that our truest self is protected by and cocooned in Christ's glorified state.

Another transformative truth is that through Christ, we share in His **Victory Over Death**. This victory is not just about physical death but encompasses all forms of spiritual death and decay. In Christ, we live a life that death cannot touch, a life that is eternal and filled with His resurrection power.

Finally, it's essential to grasp that we are not just made better but made perfect through our union with Christ. Our **Righteousness and Perfection in Christ** is a gift, not something we could achieve on our own. This perfection is the perfection of Christ Himself, shared with us through our faith in Him, making us perfect in the eyes of God.

REFLECTIVE QUESTIONS

1. How does understanding your identity as a new

creation in Christ change your daily perspective on challenges and interactions?
2. What aspects of your old life do you find challenging to consider as truly 'passed away'? How can you more fully embrace your new identity?
3. How can the concept of being 'superior' to your old self through spiritual rebirth influence your personal goals and spiritual growth?
4. In what ways can you practically apply the truth that you are freed from sin and sickness in your health and spiritual walk?
5. How does the reality of your life being hidden with Christ in God influence your sense of security and purpose in life?

Actionable Steps

- **Cultivate a Daily Awareness**: Cultivate a daily consciousness of your new identity in Christ by starting each day with a declaration of your status as a new creation. This will help reinforce your spiritual rebirth and its implications.
- **Equip Yourself with Scriptural Truths**: Equip yourself by memorizing scriptures like Romans 6:4 and 2 Corinthians 5:17 that affirm your new life and identity in Christ. This will strengthen your faith and ability to counter doubts or lies about your old self.
- **Engage in Community Reflection**: Engage with a community of believers to discuss and reflect on the meaning of being a new creation. Sharing insights

and experiences can deepen understanding and provide support in walking out this new life.

JOURNALING Prompt

Reflect on the changes in your life since you embraced your identity as a new creation in Christ. What old things have passed away? How are you experiencing the 'all things have become new' in your daily life?

THE DAY YOU BECAME ALIVE

CHAPTER 9
MADE PERFECT

Embrace the new life and identity you have in Christ. You are no longer defined by your past but by God's love and the righteousness of Christ. Stand firm in this truth and let it guide you every day.

"Therefore, if anyone is in Christ, he is a new creation; old things have passed away; behold, all things have become new." - 2 Corinthians 5:17 NKJV

In Chapter 9 titled "Made Perfect," we delve into the profound theological truth that through Christ, we have been brought from a state of imperfection, marked by sin and death, to one of complete perfection. As the author, I want to guide you through this transformative reality that began with a grave issue—the **Problem of Sin**. Since Adam's sin, all of humanity was bound to a flow of death, a relentless stream that no human effort could divert. This is the backdrop against which the entire narrative of redemption unfolds.

The old covenant, which was established through Moses, was a stopgap measure, a **Substitutionary Measure** that temporarily halted the flow of death but could not eradicate sin's power permanently. The old covenant was **Insufficient**, a fact underscored in Hebrews 10:1. It was like a placeholder, revealing the contours of something much greater that was to come. It highlighted our dire need for a perfect solution to bridge the gap between God and man.

The arrival of Jesus marked the turning point in this divine drama. He was the only one capable of resolving the sin issue completely. In a **Supernatural, Prophetic Prayer** in the upper room, revealed in John 17:23, Jesus prayed not only for His immediate disciples but for all believers, emphasizing His purpose—to make us perfect through unity with Him and the Father. Herein lies the central theme of our new covenant in Christ—through Him, we are **Made Perfect**. This perfection is not about moral impeccability but a legal and relational restoration to how God originally intended us to be.

Jesus' work on the cross introduced us to a new way of being, one where we are seen as **Complete in Him**. Colossians 2:9-10 doesn't merely suggest that we have been improved; it declares that in Christ, the fullness of the Godhead resides bodily, and we are filled in Him. This completeness means that in Christ, there is no deficiency; believers are fully equipped with everything necessary for life and godliness.

Hebrews 7:28 and 10:14 extend this concept by explaining that Jesus, who was **Perfected Forever**, has extended this perfection to us. This is a revolutionary idea because it lifts the burden of attaining perfection through human effort and places it squarely on Christ's one sacrificial act. As believers, our **Identity as Perfect in Christ** is both a present reality and an eternal truth. This identity remains intact regardless of our human failings or sins.

Understanding our new identity in Christ has practical implications for how we live our daily lives. It should influence how we view ourselves, resisting the **Condemnation of Satan** that seeks to persuade us we are anything less than what God has made us to be. It empowers us to live lives that reflect our new nature—**Righteous, Perfect, and Complete**.

Moreover, this truth has **Implications for Daily Living**, where knowing we are perfect in Christ shapes our response to temptation and sin. It is not a license to sin but a powerful motivator to live in a manner that is consistent with our new, holy nature. We are called to reflect on our spiritual reality, that in every moment, whether we succeed or fail, our fundamental nature remains unchanged because of Christ's work.

Finally, the reality of being made perfect affects **All Aspects of Life**. It reaches beyond spiritual and moral dimensions and extends to our physical well-being. The truth that we are no longer connected to sin but to Christ means that the effects of sin, which include sickness and death, no longer have a legal right to operate in our lives.

As we walk through this chapter, I invite you to embrace this truth: In Christ, you are a new creation, not just slightly improved, but wholly remade. Your connection to the first Adam has been severed, and now you are connected to Christ, the Perfect One. This is not just theological rhetoric; it is the reality of your new life in Christ. Embrace this truth, live by it, and let it transform every area of your life.

Reflective Questions

1. How does your understanding of being made perfect in Christ influence your approach to personal failures and sins?
2. In what ways can the realization that you are 'complete in Him' change your prayer life and spiritual aspirations?
3. How does knowing you are perfect in Christ affect your identity and self-worth when compared to societal standards of perfection?
4. What are practical ways you can manifest the truth of your completeness in Christ in your daily interactions and decisions?
5. How does the truth that you are perpetually perfect in Christ comfort you in times of spiritual struggle or doubt?

Actionable Steps

- **Cultivate a Consciousness of Perfection**: Regularly meditate on scriptures that affirm your completeness and perfection in Christ, such as Hebrews 10:14 and Colossians 2:9-10, to deepen your understanding and acceptance of this truth.
- **Equip Yourself with Knowledge**: Study the theological foundations of your identity in Christ to better articulate and defend this aspect of your faith, both to yourself in times of doubt and to others in discussions or evangelism.

- **Engage in Confession and Testimony**: Share the truth of your perfect state in Christ with other believers as a form of encouragement and affirmation. Use your testimony to uplift others who may struggle with feelings of inadequacy or condemnation.

Journaling Prompt

Reflect on the concept of being 'made perfect forever' as stated in Hebrews 10:14. How does this understanding change your view of God's expectations for you and your personal spiritual journey? Consider writing a prayer of thanksgiving for the perfect work of Christ that has been applied to your life.

MADE PERFECT

CHAPTER 10
FILLED WITH LIFE

Embrace the new life and identity you have in Christ. You are no longer defined by your past but by God's love and the righteousness of Christ. Stand firm in this truth and let it guide you every day.

> "Therefore, if anyone is in Christ, he is a new creation; old things have passed away; behold, all things have become new." - 2 Corinthians 5:17 NKJV

In "Filled with Life," we explore the profound transformation from death to life, a theme central to understanding our restored relationship with God through Christ. As the author, I invite you to journey back to the beginning, where **The Original Design** by God for man was to live in His image, imbued with righteousness and vibrantly alive with His very essence. This was the pinnacle of creation, where man was not only made like God but was **filled with life**, a life marked by spiritual vitality and divine fellowship.

However, the tragic shift occurred when Adam sinned, leading to an immediate and catastrophic outcome—spiritual death. This was not a mere allegorical death but a real and palpable **Consequence of Sin**, disconnecting mankind from the life of God and subjecting all creation to decay and death. From this pivotal moment, the need for restoration, for redemption, became apparent.

God, in His infinite wisdom and mercy, did not leave humanity in a state of despair. Right from the onset of mankind's fall, **The Promise of Redemption** was pronounced in Genesis 3:15. This was the first glimpse of hope, foretelling the coming of Jesus, who would crush the serpent's head, symbolizing the ultimate defeat of sin and death. This promise set the stage for the most significant event in human history—the coming of Jesus, the Last Adam, who would restore what the first had lost.

Jesus, the Last Adam, is pivotal in God's plan for humanity. Unlike the first Adam, who brought death through disobedience, Jesus, through His obedience and sacrifice, became a **life-giving spirit**. This role of Jesus was to reverse the curse of sin and death, reinstating the life that was lost in Eden. Through Him, we are offered a new covenant, a **Covenant of Life**, which is far superior to the old as it is based not on adherence to the law but on the indwelling presence of God's Spirit.

This life is not a metaphorical concept but the actual **Life of God (Zoe)**, a Greek term that encompasses more than mere physical or eternal existence—it's the qualitative, divine life that now resides in believers. When Jesus came, He did not come merely to repair our moral failings; He came to instill within us this 'zoe', transforming us from the inside out.

Having this life within us is an incredible privilege and

responsibility. It means that as believers, we have direct **Access to Divine Life**. This divine life radically alters our position before God—from alienation due to sin to intimate union with Him. Moreover, this life is not meant to be stagnant; it is meant to be evident and active within us, a **Manifestation of Life in Believers** that influences every aspect of our being—spirit, soul, and body.

Central to this continuous flow of divine life is the **Indwelling Spirit**. Romans 8:11 reassures us that the same Spirit that raised Christ from the dead lives in us, energizing and revitalizing our mortal bodies. This is not just a theological truth but a practical reality that impacts how we live daily, how we heal, and how we overcome life's challenges.

Furthermore, the **Eternal Impact of Divine Life** extends beyond individual benefits—it is designed to flow through us to others. This life is not just for our consumption but for contribution. As we carry this life, we are equipped to bring healing, restoration, and witness to the power of God's kingdom active in the world today.

In embracing this chapter, you are called to a deeper awareness and active engagement with this life. It's about realizing that you are a carrier of God's divine essence, empowered to overcome darkness and decay. This life challenges us to live not as victims of circumstance but as victors through the indwelling power of the Holy Spirit.

REFLECTIVE QUESTIONS

1. How does understanding your creation in the image of God with His life impact your view of self-worth and purpose?
2. In what ways does the life of Jesus as the Last Adam

influence your understanding of redemption and restoration?
3. How can you more actively engage with the life of God (zoe) that resides within you?
4. What changes might you need to make in your life to better reflect the divine life you carry?
5. How does the promise that the same Spirit that raised Jesus lives in you alter your expectations for healing and miracles in your life?

Actionable Steps

- **Cultivate a Deeper Relationship with the Holy Spirit**: Engage in daily prayer and meditation to foster a closer relationship with the Holy Spirit. Acknowledge His presence and ask Him to make the life of God more real and active in your daily experiences.
- **Equip Yourself with Knowledge of the Word**: Study scriptures that speak about the life of God and our new identity in Christ. This knowledge will reinforce your understanding and ability to live out this divine life.
- **Engage in Sharing the Gospel of Life**: Share the truth of this divine life with others. Testify about how this life has transformed you and offer to pray for others, believing for the life of God to manifest in their circumstances as well.

JOURNALING Prompt

Reflect on the transformation from death to life through Christ's sacrifice. How does this understanding change how you live daily? Write about ways you have noticed the life of God manifesting in your personal experiences.

FILLED WITH LIFE

CHAPTER 11
THE FLOW IN YOU

Embrace the life of God within you. Recognize that you carry the divine power that raised Christ from the dead within your spirit. Let this truth empower you daily as you walk in health and spiritual vitality.

"He who believes in Me, as the Scripture has said, out of his heart will flow rivers of living water." - John 7:38 NKJV

In Chapter 11, "The Flow in You," we delve into the fascinating structure of our being, which is intricately designed by God. Understanding that we are a **Three-Part Being**—comprised of spirit, soul, and body—is foundational. As the author, I want to guide you through this realization, emphasizing how crucial it is for the spirit, infused with God's life, to govern the soul and the body. This **Dominion of the Spirit** ensures that we operate as God intended, with our spiritual health directly influencing our physical and emotional states.

The creation narrative in Genesis 2:7 reveals a significant moment when **Life-Giving Breath** was bestowed upon man. Here, we see that man's body was initially dormant, only springing to life upon receiving the breath of life from God. This vivid illustration shows that life originates in the spirit—powered by divine breath—and from there, it permeates the body. It's essential to grasp this concept: our bodies are designed to respond to the spirit. This **Body's Response to the Spirit** is not just a biological reaction but a divine ordinance.

As we explore the interactions of Jesus, particularly in John 4 with the Samaritan woman, we encounter the profound metaphor of **Jesus as the Living Water.** His discourse about the water He offers, which leads to eternal life, illustrates that the divine gift He provides is meant to rejuvenate and sustain us eternally. This water, once received, turns into a **Fountain of Life** within us, a never-ending source that continuously revitalizes our spirit, soul, and body.

This spiritual substance, once given, is not merely a temporary aid but a **Permanence of the Gift** that embeds itself within our spirit, becoming a part of our very essence. This internal fountain is not meant to remain static; it is a **Continual Fountain** from which life perpetually flows. This internal dynamics not only redefine our spiritual existence but also enhance our physical wellbeing, linking **Salvation and Divine Health** in a way that transcends conventional understanding.

Through salvation, the **Power Within** us—spoken of by Paul in Ephesians and Romans—is the same formidable force that raised Christ from the dead. This power is not remote; it resides within us, ready to influence our physical reality, restoring health and imparting strength. Recognizing this power involves a shift in perception, a **Revelation of Life Within**, which when fully grasped, transforms our approach to health, challenges, and the impact we can have on others.

As we embrace this chapter, I encourage you to engage deeply with the concept that God's life flows within you. This isn't just about knowing it intellectually but experiencing and demonstrating it practically. The life you carry isn't meant to be hidden or dormant; it's designed to flow from you, bringing healing and wholeness to those around you. This understanding should embolden you, as it aligns you more closely with God's original plan for humanity—a plan where His life continually flows through us, transforming everything it touches.

Reflective Questions

1. How can recognizing yourself as a three-part being with the spirit in control change how you manage stress and health?
2. What practical steps can you take to ensure your spirit remains dominant over your soul and body?
3. How does Jesus' description of the living water influence your understanding of the life of God within you?
4. In what ways can you cultivate a deeper awareness of the eternal life flowing within you?
5. How can the knowledge that the same power that raised Christ dwells in you affect your daily life and interactions?

Actionable Steps

- **Cultivate Spiritual Dominance**: Prioritize spiritual practices that strengthen your spirit, such as prayer,

fasting, and meditative reading of the Scriptures, to ensure it remains dominant over your soul and body.
- **Equip with Knowledge**: Continuously educate yourself about the nature of God's life within you through Bible study and theological resources, deepening your understanding of this divine indwelling.
- **Engage in Life-Giving Activities**: Actively engage in activities that manifest the life of God through you, such as healing ministry, prophetic prayer, and acts of kindness, demonstrating the flow of divine life in and through your life.

Journaling **Prompt**

Reflect on the recent times when you have felt the life of God actively working in your life. How did it manifest? Consider situations where you experienced physical renewal, emotional peace, or spiritual insight. Write about these experiences and how they affirm the reality of God's life flowing through you.

THE FLOW IN YOU

CHAPTER 12
WHO DO YOU THINK YOU ARE?

Believe in your new identity in Christ. Knowing who you are in Him empowers you to live beyond the limitations of the natural world and step into the supernatural life He intended for you.

"For He made Him who knew no sin to be sin for us, that we might become the righteousness of God in Him." - 2 Corinthians 5:21 NKJV

In Chapter 12, "Who Do You Think You Are?", I explore the profound implications of our identity in Christ. Understanding and embracing this identity is more than a theological concept; it is the foundation of our spiritual existence and empowerment. The struggle with identity is not new. **Satan's Primary Target** has always been our identity, as shown from the very beginning in the Garden of Eden. He tempted Eve by questioning her identity, which was already like God's, created in His image and likeness.

The power of identity is vividly illustrated in the **Temptation of Jesus** in the wilderness. Here, Satan's challenge to Jesus was an attack on His sonship, His identity. But unlike Eve, Jesus knew who He was and thus did not succumb to Satan's lies. His response provides a blueprint for us: knowing your identity in Christ shields you against the enemy's attacks and empowers you to live out your God-given destiny.

2 Corinthians 5:17 marks a pivotal verse for every believer. It proclaims that in Christ, we are a new creation; old things have passed away, and all things have become new. This new creation is not just about moral improvement but a total transformation into a new identity—spiritually reborn, free from the curse, and living a supernatural lifestyle.

Not by Appearance—we learn to no longer regard anyone according to the flesh. This principle teaches us that our true identity is not reflected by our physical appearance or our past, but by our new nature in Christ. As believers, our real identity is hidden in Him. We mirror Jesus' life not only through His resurrection but also in His ongoing life in heaven.

Living as a New Creation means understanding that we are now spirit beings, meant to live a life powered by the spirit. Our identity is not defined by our physical circumstances but by our spiritual reality in Christ. This realization allows us to rise above the earthly and temporal and tap into the eternal and divine.

The Righteous Reality—2 Corinthians 5:21 emphasizes that we have become the righteousness of God in Christ. This is not just a title but a reality that should manifest in every area of our lives, including health and wholeness. Our healing and well-being are part of our righteous identity.

Christ in Us—our new identity means Christ lives in us, and we in Him. This union is transformative, making us partakers of His divine nature and enabling us to live beyond human limitations.

WHO DO YOU THINK YOU ARE?

Empowered by Identity—when we fully grasp our identity in Christ, it changes everything. We no longer see ourselves as mere humans struggling through life but as divine agents of God's kingdom, equipped with all the power of heaven.

REFLECTIVE QUESTIONS

1. How does understanding your identity in Christ change the way you face challenges?
2. What steps can you take to reinforce your identity as a new creation in Christ daily?
3. How does the righteousness of Christ in you influence your approach to health and healing?
4. What scriptures can you meditate on to strengthen your understanding of your divine identity?
5. In what ways can you start living out the reality of Christ in you in your community?

ACTIONABLE STEPS

- **Cultivate Your New Identity**: Spend time daily in Scripture, focusing on verses that affirm your identity in Christ, to reinforce the truth of who you are in Him.
- **Equip Yourself with Truth**: Educate yourself continually about your rights and privileges as a believer through sermons, books, and teachings that focus on identity in Christ.
- **Engage Your World as Christ Would**: Actively look for opportunities to demonstrate the life of Christ in

practical ways, such as through acts of kindness, healing prayers, and sharing the gospel, reflecting your identity as a representative of Jesus.

Journaling **Prompt**

Reflect on a recent situation where knowing your identity in Christ changed your response or perspective. Write about this experience and how it influenced the outcome. Consider how you can apply this awareness more consistently in your daily life to live from victory rather than for victory.

WHO DO YOU THINK YOU ARE?

NEVER BE SICK AGAIN OFFICIAL WORKBOOK

CHAPTER 13
RECEIVING YOUR HEALING IS FOR THE SINNER

Embrace the reality that healing is part of your identity in Christ. Recognize that the same power that resurrected Christ lives within you, offering not just spiritual rejuvenation but also physical healing.

"By whose stripes you were healed." - 1 Peter 2:24 NKJV

In Chapter 13, "Receiving Your Healing Is for the Sinner," I delve into a provocative discussion aimed to realign our understanding of healing in the Christian life. **The Distinction in Healing** between the sinner and the Christian is crucial; while the sinner seeks healing, the Christian already possesses it within, as Christ's work on the cross provided it fully.

Understanding 1 Peter 2:24 is pivotal. This scripture does not instruct Christians to seek healing; instead, it declares that healing is already an accomplished fact, a part of the new identity you have in Christ. This reflects a significant **Shift from Receiving to Releasing Healing**, emphasizing that Christians are not merely recipients but conduits of God's healing power through their identity in Christ.

The Christian's Healing Paradigm involves recognizing that the power to heal does not come from external efforts to 'receive' healing but from the realization and activation of what is already within. This understanding transforms our approach from seeking to manifesting the healing already provided by Christ's atonement.

Healing as a Done Reality, not a distant possibility, encourages us to live from victory, not for victory. When we grasp that healing is already ours, it shifts our focus from trying to obtain to simply releasing what we possess.

Ephesians 1:3 underscores that every spiritual blessing in Christ is already ours. This includes healing, which is not separated from the holistic blessings we have received in Him. **Paul's Silence on Healing Steps** in his epistles underscores that healing is not something Christians need to strive for but something to walk in, owing to our new nature in Christ.

The Identity Revelation in healing is about knowing 'who' you are more than 'how' to be healed. Teaching on healing should focus on revealing identity rather than instructing on methods. This aligns with **Walking in Who You Have Received**, emphasizing our complete union with Christ, which makes His life, including His health, ours.

Kingdom Culture of Health—Paul taught about a Kingdom where sickness is alien, emphasizing that the believer's environment in Christ is inherently devoid of disease, a profound truth that should reshape our expectations and experiences of health.

Activating the Healing Within shifts our paradigm from seeking healing to acknowledging and activating the healing available through our indwelling Spirit. This understanding liberates and empowers us to live out the fullness of our divine health.

Reflective Questions

1. How does understanding that you already possess healing change your approach to physical ailments?
2. What mental shifts need to occur in your life to move from seeking healing to releasing it?
3. How can the realization that healing is a part of your identity in Christ affect your ministry to others?
4. In what ways can you cultivate a deeper awareness of the indwelling Spirit's power within you?
5. How does the revelation of being a 'releaser' of God's power change your daily walk with God?

Actionable Steps

- **Cultivate an Awareness of the Indwelling Spirit:** Regularly meditate on scriptures that affirm the presence and power of the Holy Spirit within you, strengthening your consciousness of His active presence.
- **Equip Yourself with Kingdom Truths:** Immerse yourself in teachings and resources that affirm the Kingdom's culture of health and wholeness, reinforcing your understanding of your rights and realities in Christ.
- **Engage in Faith-Filled Declarations:** Speak healing and wholeness over your life and others, practicing

the release of God's power through your words and actions, as an expression of the divine life within you.

JOURNALING Prompt

Reflect on a time when you experienced or witnessed healing. How did that moment align with your understanding of healing being part of your identity in Christ? Journal about how this perspective can be further integrated into your daily life, transforming how you view health and sickness.

∼

RECEIVING YOUR HEALING IS FOR THE SINNER

CHAPTER 14
YOU ARE THE BODY OF CHRIST

Remember, you are not just a part of the body of Christ; you embody His fullness wherever you go. Live boldly and confidently, knowing that the life of Jesus flows through you, enabling you to bring light and healing to the world.

John 15:5 NKJV: "I am the vine, you are the branches. He who abides in Me, and I in him, bears much fruit; for without Me you can do nothing."

As we journey through the understanding that **Christ as the Head** of the Church, it becomes profoundly clear that just as a body cannot function without its head, we, the church, are utterly dependent on Jesus for our direction, vitality, and purpose. This foundational truth is critical, for without acknowledging Jesus as our head, we lose our life force and direction. It's essential to grasp that in this spiritual organism, every believer plays a pivotal role. Whether you are a teacher, a server, or a prayer warrior, you are part of a divine tapestry.

Individual and Collective Identity are vital aspects of our faith walk. You and I are not the entire body ourselves; rather, we are individual members of a much larger entity composed of countless believers worldwide. It is truly inspiring to realize that as members of this vast body, our individual contributions, no matter how small they may seem, are crucial to the overall health and function of the Church. This understanding should bring a profound sense of belonging and purpose to each of us. Recognizing our role within this collective helps us appreciate the diversity and the unity that we share in Christ.

In considering the significance of every part of a human body, it's clear that both the seen and unseen parts are necessary for the body's health and functionality. The same is true for the body of Christ; every member is important. The **Importance of Every Member** cannot be overstated—each role, whether prominent or behind the scenes, contributes to the effectiveness of the whole. Just as every cell and organ in a human body is vital, every believer is essential in the spiritual body of Christ. Understanding this can transform how we view ourselves and others within the church, fostering a more inclusive and supportive community.

Connection to the Head is a vivid reminder that just as limbs and organs must be connected to the brain to function, we must remain connected to Christ, our Head, to thrive spiritually. This connection is our lifeline, the source from which we draw our spiritual sustenance and strength. No matter what role we play, our spiritual vitality and effectiveness stem from our connection to Jesus. Embracing this truth enables us to live powerfully and purposefully, knowing that the life of Christ flows through us.

The scripture in John 1:16, "And of His fullness we have all received, and grace for grace," underscores that **Fullness of Christ in Believers** is a profound reality. This fullness is not partial or limited; it is a complete infusion of His life and power into us. Realizing that you carry the fullness of Him wherever you go can revolutionize your faith experience and your impact on the world. This fullness equips you to face challenges, overcome obstacles, and extend the kingdom of God on Earth through both natural and supernatural expressions of His love and power.

As believers, we are called not only to live ordinary lives but to be **Active Extensions of Jesus** on this Earth. This extends beyond simple acts of kindness to include the supernatural workings that reflect Jesus' ministry. If Jesus healed the sick, cast out demons, and calmed storms, and we are His body, then isn't it logical that we too are empowered to do these things? This perspective is vital because it moves us from seeing ourselves as mere followers to being active participants in His divine mission. Each of us is equipped to carry forward the miraculous, life-changing power of Jesus.

Divine Health and Authority are not just theological concepts but realities that you and I are meant to experience and manifest. Just as Jesus walked this earth in divine health, free from sin and sickness, so are we called to embody this divine nature. We are to be conduits of His power, demonstrating that the life flowing from the Head, Jesus, into His body, the Church, is devoid of sickness and sin. This understanding compels us to live in a manner that is radically different from the world, showcasing the kingdom of God through our lives.

It's time for a paradigm shift in our spiritual lives. The call to change the **Changing Church Perspectives** on how we address both sin and sickness is urgent. We often vigorously oppose sin, as we should, but do we battle sickness with the same fervor? As the body of Christ, empowered by the Head, we must adopt a stance that sees sickness in the same light as sin—a foreign element that has no place in our lives. This shift will not only bring about healing in the physical but will also restore a sense of spiritual authority and victory within the church.

Rejection of Passivity in our spiritual practice is crucial. We must move beyond merely asking for God's presence to actively acknowledging and utilizing the divine connection we have with Jesus. We are not bystanders in our faith; we are branches grafted into the Vine, continually nourished and sustained by His life. This proactive stance in our spiritual lives encourages us to engage more deeply with our faith, transforming our prayers, worship, and daily interactions.

Finally, the recognition that we are meant to be **Empowerment to Transform** agents in this world is essential. As extensions of Jesus, endowed with His power and authority, our calling is not just to survive in this world but to transform it. You carry within you the potential to effect real change, to bring healing where there is hurt, and light where there is darkness. The power that raised Christ from the dead is the same power that works within us, calling us to rise up and live out the fullness of our divine inheritance.

Reflective Questions

1. How do you perceive your role within the body of Christ, and how can you better fulfill this role based on your unique gifts?
2. In what ways have you experienced the fullness of Christ in your daily life, and how can this awareness influence your interactions with others?
3. What steps can you take to enhance your connection

to Christ, ensuring His life and power flow more freely in your actions?
4. How can the church's approach to dealing with sin and sickness be aligned more closely with the authority we have in Christ?
5. What are the practical implications of seeing yourself as an active extension of Jesus, especially in contexts that require supernatural intervention?

Actionable Steps

- **Cultivate a Deeper Relationship with Christ**: Spend time daily in prayer and meditation on the Scriptures to strengthen your connection to Jesus, the Head of the Church. This will enhance your sensitivity to His guidance and the flow of His life within you.
- **Equip Yourself with Knowledge of Your Authority in Christ**: Study biblical teachings and resources that explain the believer's authority over sin and sickness. Understanding your spiritual rights and capacities is crucial for living out your divine mandate.
- **Engage in Kingdom Activities**: Actively participate in both church-based and individual outreach activities that demonstrate the kingdom of God, especially those that involve healing, prophecy, and other supernatural ministries. This not only affirms your role as part of the body of Christ but also extends its healing and transformative power to others.

JOURNALING Prompt

Reflect on a recent situation where you felt disconnected from the life and power of Christ. What were the circumstances, and how might a deeper awareness of your identity as part of His body have changed your approach and outcome? Consider ways to maintain and strengthen this connection in future challenges.

YOU ARE THE BODY OF CHRIST

CHAPTER 15
DON'T GET CHEATED

Remember, as believers, we are equipped with every spiritual blessing in heavenly places; do not let deceptive teachings or human traditions rob you of your inheritance. Stand firm in the truth that in Christ, you are complete and fully equipped for every good work.

Colossians 2:10 NKJV: "And you are complete in Him, who is the head of all principality and power."

In our exploration of how believers can be spiritually cheated, we uncover a crucial reality: **Spiritual Cheating is Real**. Many of us, perhaps unknowingly, miss out on the full blessings that are rightfully ours. This often happens not through outright theft, but through subtle deceptions—worldly philosophies and empty deceits that masquerade as benign or even beneficial. These deceptions can strip away the fullness of the inheritance that Christ has secured for us, leaving us spiritually impoverished when we were meant to live in abundance.

As followers of Christ, we are heirs to an **Inheritance of Spiritual Blessings**; Ephesians 1:3 tells us that we have been blessed with every spiritual blessing in the heavenly places in Christ. This assurance is profound—it means every resource, every blessing that Heaven can offer, is ours. Realizing this should empower us to live fully and effectively, free from the lies of insufficiency that the world tries to impose on us.

One of the most empowering aspects of our faith is understanding that we are **Complete in Christ**. According to Colossians 2:10, in Him, we are made whole, possessing everything we need for life and godliness. This completeness is a present reality, not a distant goal. It challenges every notion of deficiency and empowers us to live from a place of divine sufficiency.

However, this understanding can often be clouded by the **Dangers of Human Philosophy and Traditions**. These elements, rooted in human reasoning and not divine revelation, can dilute the potency of our faith. They distract us from the simplicity and power of the gospel, leading to spiritual stagnation and regression.

In every area of our lives, **Christ as the Standard** must prevail. He exemplifies what it means to live a life fully yielded to God's will. Anything less than this fullness is settling for less than what His sacrifice intended for us. This standard calls us to live lives of profound spiritual and moral integrity, striving to mirror His example in our daily actions.

The **Potential for Misinterpretation** of scripture is a significant risk, especially when approached without a relational understanding of Christ. Intellectual knowledge or familiarity with biblical texts does not equate to true wisdom or insight. Instead, our approach to the Bible should be relational, seeking to know Christ deeply and allowing His Spirit to reveal the true meaning of His words.

The comfort of familiar **The Trap of Traditionalism** can become a barrier to deeper spiritual insight. Traditions, even those deeply rooted in church history, must be continually evaluated against the immutable truth of Scripture. They should enhance, not hinder, our relationship with Christ.

Choosing to **Live Counter-Culturally** means embracing biblical truths over societal norms, especially concerning health, aging, and ethical integrity. We are called to defy worldly expectations and live according to God's standards, which often requires us to stand apart from contemporary cultural norms.

Divine Health as a Covenant Right is another profound truth. Like Moses, who climbed Mount Nebo at one hundred twenty with full strength and vision, we too are called to a life of divine health and vitality. This promise stands in stark contrast to the world's resignation to decay and decline as parts of aging or life.

Finally, embracing **Heaven's Normal** means rejecting the world's definitions of normalcy. What the world accepts as inevitable—sickness, decay, and defeat—should be foreign to us. We are called to live by the standards of Heaven, where fullness of life, health, and vitality are the norm, not the exception.

Reflective Questions

1. How do you currently protect yourself from being spiritually cheated by worldly philosophies and human traditions?
2. In what ways can you more fully embrace your inheritance of spiritual blessings?

3. What does being "complete in Christ" practically mean to you in your daily life?
4. How can you ensure your understanding of Scripture is deeply rooted in a relationship with Christ rather than just intellectual knowledge?
5. How can the standard of Christ's life challenge and enhance your personal and spiritual growth?

ACTIONABLE STEPS

- **Cultivate a Relationship with Christ**: Spend daily time in prayer and meditation on Scripture, seeking to deepen your relationship with Christ and ensuring your life aligns with His teachings.
- **Equip Yourself with Knowledge**: Regularly study the promises of spiritual blessings and completeness in Christ, empowering yourself with the knowledge to combat any spiritual deceit.
- **Engage in Community Discernment**: Participate in community discussions or Bible study groups where you can collectively discern and challenge traditional beliefs and cultural norms against the truth of Scripture.

JOURNALING **Prompt**

Reflect on a time when you felt pressured by traditional or cultural norms that conflicted with your understanding of what it means to be complete in Christ. How did you respond, and what did you learn from that experience?

DON'T GET CHEATED

CHAPTER 16
OUR BELIEF IN SICKNESS

Remember, as believers, we are not only saved from sin but from every curse, including sickness. Our belief systems need to align with the truths of Scripture, not the norms of a fallen world. Embrace the fullness of health that is your inheritance in Christ.

"And do not be conformed to this world, but be transformed by the renewing of your mind, that you may prove what is that good and acceptable and perfect will of God." Romans 12:2 NKJV:

In this chapter, we delve into a crucial aspect of our spiritual lives that often goes overlooked—our beliefs concerning health and sickness. It's vital to recognize that **The Power of Belief** significantly shapes our experience in the physical realm. What we believe, whether consciously or unconsciously, can dictate whether we walk in divine health or remain susceptible to illness. Many believers operate from a position of defense, reacting to sickness when it arises, rather than standing firm in the offensive posture that our inheritance in Christ allows. This **Defensive vs. Offensive Healing** approach highlights a key area where we need a paradigm shift. We must transition from merely defending against sickness to actively affirming and walking in the health and wholeness that are norms in the Kingdom of Heaven.

The norms we often accept concerning health are deeply influenced by the world around us. However, as believers, we are called to align our standards not with **Worldly Norms vs. Kingdom Realities** but with the realities of where Christ is in Heaven. This stark contrast between the world's acceptance of sickness as inevitable and the Kingdom's provision of complete health is foundational. By **Renewing the Mind**, as Paul instructs in Romans 12:2, we start the transformation process, allowing God's truth to reshape our thinking and, consequently, our living. This renewal helps us to manifest God's perfect will on earth, proving in practice that His plans for us are not only good but are aimed towards our true maturity and well-being.

Understanding **Heaven's Will on Earth** is crucial. The will of God in Heaven—total health and freedom from sickness—is also His will for us here on earth. This divine will is proven as we realign our thoughts and beliefs with the realities of Heaven, which declare divine health as our portion. However, this truth faces opposition from the pervasive **Cultural Conditioning** that normalizes sickness and deterioration with age. As part of the body of Christ, we must actively reject this conditioning, embracing instead the robust health that Jesus has provided through His atonement.

In many church teachings, there is an undue focus on managing sickness rather than living in the robust health that is our right as believers. This focus on **The Role of Teaching** about healing as a reactionary measure rather than a preventative or definitive state reflects a misalignment with biblical truth. Such teachings should empower believers to live in the fullness of health, reinforcing our **Identity in Christ** as righteous and healed, exempt from the curse of sickness.

Our **Spiritual Authority** over sickness is a significant aspect of our identity in Christ. Living from this authority fundamentally changes our experience of life, shifting us from victims to victors. This authority allows us to reject sickness proactively, affirming our God-given health. Furthermore, understanding that **Healing as a Right** is not just a possibility but a covenantal promise is essential. As heirs with Christ, complete health is not just an option—it is our inheritance.

REFLECTIVE QUESTIONS

1. How have your beliefs about health been shaped by cultural norms rather than biblical truths?
2. In what ways can you shift from a defensive to an offensive approach to health and healing?
3. What steps can you take to renew your mind to align with the reality of Heaven's health?
4. How does understanding your identity in Christ as righteous and healed change your approach to sickness?
5. How can you exercise your spiritual authority to maintain health and combat sickness?

Actionable Steps

- **Cultivate a Kingdom Mindset:** Spend time daily meditating on Scriptures that affirm your health and healing in Christ to build a strong belief in divine health.
- **Equip Yourself with Knowledge:** Educate yourself on what the Bible says about healing and health. Understanding your rights and privileges in Christ is key to living them out.
- **Engage in Proactive Health Declarations:** Start each day by declaring your health and healing in Christ. Speak life over your body and reject any agreement with sickness.

Journaling Prompt

Reflect on how you have viewed health and sickness up to this point. Consider any negative beliefs you've held about your health that align more with worldly views than with the truth of Scripture. How can you begin to shift these beliefs to align with your identity in Christ?

OUR BELIEF IN SICKNESS

CHAPTER 17
A NEW KINGDOM

Let's embrace the truth that in Christ, we are set completely free —not just from sin, but from all its consequences, including sickness. As citizens of Heaven, Heaven's normal is our normal. This means living in health as a reflection of the kingdom we belong to.

Colossians 1:13-14 TPT "He has rescued us completely from the tyrannical rule of darkness and has translated us into the kingdom realm of his beloved Son. For in the Son all our sins are canceled and we have the release of redemption through his very blood."

As we navigate our lives on earth, it's vital to recognize our true **citizenship in God's Kingdom,** where sickness and disease are foreign concepts. This profound realization opens us to an **over the top, almost too good to be true salvation** that not only rescues us from darkness but also wholly integrates us into a realm where our sins are absolved and redemption is our daily reality. Our present existence isn't about waiting for the afterlife to experience the Kingdom; we are **living in it now**, manifesting Heaven's standards on earth.

The normalcy of Heaven—where pain, illness, and poverty are nonexistent—is meant to be our norm too. As such, **Heaven's standards on earth** should dictate our expectations and experiences, especially regarding health. To actualize this, the Apostle Paul urges us to **renew our minds**, moving our focus from earthly to heavenly realities. This renewal is transformative, aligning our physical reality with our spiritual standing in Christ.

Understanding our **disconnection from sin and its byproducts** through Christ's sacrifice underscores that diseases, as sin's outcomes, hold no authority over us. Our **spiritual reality affects our physical reality**—since we are liberated from sin, its associated ailments like sickness should not plague us. This is a radical shift from the earthly acceptance that aging involves decline and disease. Instead, as kingdom citizens, the notion that **the older you get, the sicker you get** should appear entirely foreign to us.

The call to challenge these **earthly norms** about health and age is not just theoretical but a practical, daily declaration of our freedom in Christ. The biblical account of Moses, who did not succumb to sickness but departed life in robust health, exemplifies this **Kingdom reality of health**. Such scriptural narratives reinforce that we should not expect or accept illness as part of our lives.

Furthermore, our dialogue and thoughts about diseases like cancer often reveal deep-seated fears that contradict our kingdom identity. **Fear and belief** in such illnesses are out of place in the lives of those who embody God's kingdom on earth.

Every mention of a disease that brings a twinge of fear challenges us to reassess our faith's alignment with kingdom truths.

By internalizing and living out these truths, we pave the way not only for our well-being but for a testament to the world of what it means to live under God's reign. This transformation begins in the heart and mind, where our beliefs shape our health and our experience of God's kingdom here on earth. As we embrace this heavenly citizenship, let's engage with every opportunity to manifest this divine health and challenge the status quo, bringing light to the shadowed places of worldly acceptance of disease and decay.

Reflective Questions

1. How have your own beliefs about health been shaped by worldly standards?
2. What steps can you take to align your health beliefs more closely with Kingdom realities?
3. In what ways have you experienced the health of Heaven on earth?
4. How does the community around you reflect or contradict the health standards of God's Kingdom?
5. What practical changes can you make to foster a Kingdom-focused environment in your personal and community life?

Actionable Steps

- **Cultivate** a daily declaration of your health in Christ

by affirming your freedom from sickness as part of your morning routine.
- **Equip** yourself with scriptures that promise divine health and meditate on them regularly to build your faith.
- **Engage** in community discussions that promote Kingdom truths about health, challenging common misconceptions and fears about sickness.

Journaling Prompt

Reflect on your current health beliefs and write about how they align or differ from the truths of God's Kingdom. Explore how changing your perspective might affect your physical and mental well-being.

A NEW KINGDOM

NEVER BE SICK AGAIN OFFICIAL WORKBOOK

CHAPTER 18
SUBSTITUTING BRASS FOR GOLD

Embrace the reality that you are called to manifest God's healing power not just within the church walls but predominantly to those outside, the unsaved and the hurting. This aligns with the original intent of the Great Commission, which compels us to be active agents of God's miraculous power in the world.

Mark 16:18 NKJV "And these signs will follow those who believe: In My name they will cast out demons; they will speak with new tongues; they will take up serpents; and if they drink anything deadly, it will by no means hurt them; they will lay hands on the sick, and they will recover."

In our journey through the scriptures and **the Great Commission**, we find a clear directive from Jesus Christ. This command is not just about preaching but also demonstrating the Kingdom through healing. It is crucial to understand that **the primary audience for these miraculous**

signs was the unsaved. This focus helps clarify our mission in the world, which is to extend the healing touch of Jesus to those who have not yet encountered Him.

The early church's approach was to lay hands predominantly on sinners as a testimony of God's power and mercy. This was intended as a sign to unbelievers, confirming the gospel's truth and power. Yet, today, we often see a different pattern, with believers primarily ministering healing to one another. This shift begs a significant question about our alignment with biblical teachings and the **original purpose of healing** in the church's ministry.

Reflecting on the New Testament, we find that healing among believers was exceptionally rare and typically reserved for life-threatening conditions or as a powerful sign of God's immediate intervention, such as when Peter raised Tabitha or Paul raised Eutychus. These instances were not the norm but rather extraordinary events that underscored the apostles' authority and God's overriding power over death.

The **call to return to scriptural fidelity** in our healing ministry is urgent. By refocusing our efforts on reaching the unsaved with healing, we align more closely with the New Testament model. This involves a shift from a predominantly inward-looking approach to an outward, evangelistic strategy that uses healing as a bridge to convey the gospel's message to the unchurched.

Restoring the focus of our healing ministry requires us to equip and empower the church body comprehensively. This includes teaching believers about their authority in Christ and encouraging them to exercise this authority not just within the church but as a witness to the world. By doing so, we not only adhere to Christ's commands but also activate the church in its primary role as a light to the nations.

In conclusion, our challenge today is to shift from substituting brass for gold—settling for less than what God has intended. We are called to aim for the highest—living out the fullness of our mandate to bring God's kingdom on earth as it is in heaven, particularly through the ministry of healing. By realigning our practices with biblical precedents, we will not only uphold the truth of the gospel but also demonstrate its power in the most compelling ways possible.

REFLECTIVE QUESTIONS

1. How can we better align our healing ministry with the New Testament model?
2. What steps can we take to ensure that our church focuses on reaching the unsaved with healing?
3. In what ways have we seen the power of healing testify to the truth of the gospel in our community?
4. How can we encourage believers to exercise their authority in Christ more effectively?
5. What changes need to be made in our approach to healing ministry to reflect more of Christ's intent rather than our traditions?

ACTIONABLE STEPS

- **Cultivate a deeper understanding** of the Great Commission as it relates to healing.
- **Equip every believer** with the knowledge and faith to exercise their authority in healing.
- **Engage the unsaved** with acts of healing as a testament to the gospel's power.

JOURNALING **Prompt**

Reflect on your experiences with healing, either receiving or ministering it. How have these moments aligned with or deviated from the biblical examples? What steps can you take to more fully embrace your role in God's healing work as outlined in the scriptures?

SUBSTITUTING BRASS FOR GOLD

NEVER BE SICK AGAIN OFFICIAL WORKBOOK

CHAPTER 19
GENERATIONAL CURSES AND YOUR BLOODLINE

The redemption we have in Christ goes beyond what many believers realize. We are not just forgiven; we are made entirely new, severed from any curse that could be tied to our past lineage. Our union with Christ has completely transformed us, including our family line. If we truly understand our new identity and inheritance in Jesus, we will see that there is no room for fear of generational curses or anything that might be associated with our past bloodline. Christ has made us free indeed, and through Him, we are blessed, whole, and made new.

"Therefore if the Son makes you free, you shall be free indeed." (John 8:36 NKJV)

In my heart, I want every believer to understand that **our union with Christ has completely transformed us**, including our lineage and all its past associations. As followers of Jesus, we often encounter teachings about generational curses, but I must emphasize: if we truly grasp what redemption means, these teachings lose their grip. When we accepted Christ, **our bloodline was redeemed**. God became our Father, and our identity was renewed. We are no longer bound by the past, no longer tied to the curses or consequences of previous generations. Understanding that **God is now our Father** changes everything. The connection we once had with the lineage of Adam, carrying with it sin and sickness, has been replaced with a direct connection to the lineage of Christ, who defeated sin and death.

Some might wonder where these ideas of generational curses come from, as they aren't found in the New Testament teachings directed at believers. One commonly cited verse is from **Exodus 20:5**, where God warned Israel about iniquity visiting multiple generations. Yet, this verse was directed to those under the Old Covenant, a covenant that was fulfilled and transformed by Jesus. What Jesus brought us is greater than any curse; it is the **complete redemption from the curse of the law**. Through Christ, we are in a new place of freedom where the burdens of the past no longer have power over us. What some believers struggle with is not understanding this **freedom that Christ offers**, a freedom that fully covers all areas of our lives.

Imagine how much stronger and more confident we would be if we fully realized that **no curse can touch those in Christ**. It is impossible to reconcile the idea of generational curses with the promises of the New Covenant, which declare us free and redeemed. This isn't just a hopeful thought; it is a truth established by the power of the cross. As we were brought into union with Christ, **we were disconnected from sin and all its effects**. It is why I urge every believer to stop seeing themselves as tied to a lineage of defeat and instead embrace the victory and new life Jesus provides.

Another teaching that often accompanies this concept of

generational curses is the notion that we need to **redeem our bloodline**. But think about it: if Christ has redeemed us, what further redemption does our bloodline need? **God has already established our lineage** in His family through the work of Jesus, and our identity now flows from that heavenly source. We are not merely cleansed; we are reborn. Our ancestry is now traced directly to the Father Himself, eliminating any need for additional "redemption" practices.

So let me ask: why would we think **we need additional rituals or efforts** to break free from curses? The truth is, teachings about generational curses not only misunderstand our relationship with God but also undermine the power of grace. They subtly suggest that what Jesus did on the cross is not enough, that there's still something left for us to fix. But Jesus completed the work. **We are whole in Him**, lacking nothing, fully supplied by His finished work. To hold onto ideas of generational bondage is to hold onto the past and reject the freedom Christ has already provided.

We are called to a greater understanding of **our new nature in Christ**, a nature that has left all curses, all old identities, and all previous claims behind. When God sees us, He sees us through the perfect life of His Son. There is no generational curse that can stand against the power of Christ's blood. He has set us free from every bond and every tie. The same blood that saved us cleansed us completely and filled us with new life, leaving no room for fear of the past.

If you have ever worried about generational curses, I urge you to rest in the knowledge that **Christ has removed any hold the past may have had**. When we accepted Him, His righteousness became our new legacy, one that shines brighter than anything our earthly bloodline could provide. We are heirs of God, co-heirs with Christ, and our inheritance is one of life, freedom, and blessing. This is the truth that sets us free, once and for all.

Reflective Questions

1. How does understanding our union with Christ change our view of past generational influences?
2. What does it mean to have God as our Father in terms of our identity and inheritance?
3. How can focusing on our redemption in Christ help us overcome fear related to generational curses?
4. What are the implications of knowing that Jesus' blood has redeemed our entire bloodline?
5. Why might it be challenging for some believers to let go of the concept of generational curses, and how can they embrace the truth of the New Covenant?

Actionable Steps

- **Cultivate** your faith in your new identity by meditating on scriptures that affirm your union with Christ, such as Galatians 2:20.
- **Equip** yourself with understanding by studying verses that highlight your position as a child of God, ensuring that you know what Jesus' redemption fully accomplished for you.
- **Engage** with other believers by encouraging them to walk in freedom and assurance of their new nature in Christ, sharing the truth that generational curses have no place in a redeemed life.

. . .

Journaling Prompt

Reflect on what it means for God to be your Father and the beginning of your bloodline. Write about how understanding this truth affects your perspective on past family challenges and your approach to living in freedom today.

NEVER BE SICK AGAIN OFFICIAL WORKBOOK

GENERATIONAL CURSES AND YOUR BLOODLINE

CHAPTER 20
SATAN ISN'T TRESPASSING ON YOUR BODY

Remember, Satan's influence over us is limited. His power is rooted only in deception, suggestion, and lies. Our authority in Christ makes it impossible for him to trespass in our lives without our permission. By staying vigilant and standing firm in our union with Christ, we secure a life free from fear and empowered by faith. Through Christ, we are more than conquerors, equipped to resist every attempt of the enemy to draw us into anxiety or sin.

Mark 4:19 NKJV "Then the cares and anxieties of the world and distractions of the age, and the pleasure and delight and false glamour and deceitfulness of riches, and the craving and passionate desire for other things creep in and choke and suffocate the Word, and it becomes fruitless."

SATAN ISN'T TRESPASSING ON YOUR BODY

In this chapter, I want to clear up some misunderstandings about the ways Satan operates in the life of a believer. Many times, I've heard people say things like, "Satan is trespassing on my body," especially when sickness or difficulties come. This idea might seem natural, but it's crucial to understand that **Satan cannot trespass against believers without permission.** Trespassing implies entering someone's property unlawfully, without their knowledge or consent. But, as believers, we are not unguarded property. Through our union with Christ, we've been given authority that establishes clear boundaries, and it is only when we allow him to that Satan can cross those boundaries. It's empowering to understand that Satan is limited in what he can do to a person living in the authority of Christ.

Let's go back to **the Garden of Eden to understand how Satan works.** When Satan tempted Eve, he couldn't make her sin or force her to act. Instead, he relied on his usual tactic—deception. He used subtlety, suggesting she could be "like God," but the decision was entirely hers. This demonstrates that Satan operates through temptation and deception, not by forcibly making believers sin. This pattern, seen with Eve, reveals that Satan's power is limited to suggestions, and our free will is what determines the outcome. Satan doesn't hold ultimate power over us.

Jesus' encounter with Satan in the wilderness further proves Satan's limitations. When Jesus was fasting, Satan tried again to influence someone righteous, presenting temptations. He offered power, provision, and safety, but he couldn't compel Jesus to act. If Satan had the power to simply force outcomes, he would have made Jesus worship him, throw Himself down, or turn stones to bread. He didn't, because he couldn't. This shows that Satan's power over believers, who are also made righteous through Christ, is similarly limited. He can only offer thoughts, ideas, and lies.

Because of this, believers need to understand that **we have power over Satan, not the other way around**. The righteousness we have received in Christ places us in a position of authority. Satan cannot force his way into our lives or bodies. He cannot afflict us with sickness or sin without our allowance. So, when we recognize our authority, we realize Satan cannot act without us accepting or consenting to his influence.

That's why it's essential to recognize that **Satan works through lies, deceit, and suggestions**. The Bible calls him a liar, deceiver, and tempter, meaning that he operates by subtly influencing our thoughts. His objective is to plant negative thoughts and ideas, hoping we will act on them. But, by staying vigilant and discerning, we can reject anything that doesn't align with God's truth, thus preventing Satan's influence from gaining ground.

Ananias and Sapphira's story in the book of Acts illustrates Satan's tactics. They were righteous believers, yet they succumbed to the temptation to lie about their giving. Satan "filled their heart," which means he introduced the suggestion to deceive, but he didn't make them lie. They chose to act on the thought themselves. This example highlights how Satan only has the power to suggest; the choice to act is ours.

One critical point I want you to see here is that **cares and anxieties open doors to Satan's influence**. When we carry the weight of worldly worries, fears, and concerns, we unintentionally grant Satan access to influence us. Scripture tells us to cast our cares upon God, to free ourselves from anxiety. By doing this, we protect ourselves from vulnerability to Satan's influence, as cares are often what he uses to lead believers away from God's peace.

We see this illustrated with **Job's fears, which allowed**

Satan access to his life. Job lived in fear, particularly about his children, and it became a weakness that Satan exploited. This incident shows us that harboring fear and worry does not strengthen us—it weakens us spiritually and allows the enemy an entry point. That's why the Bible stresses the importance of putting our full trust in God.

As believers, **we must actively protect our peace**. In today's world, it's easy to be overwhelmed by financial worries, health concerns, family matters, and more. Yet the Bible tells us to guard our peace vigilantly. When we let go of peace and cling to cares, Satan can use these distractions to draw us into stress, doubt, or even sin. Peace acts as a spiritual shield, keeping us grounded in Christ.

Ultimately, our goal is to **identify with Christ to repel the enemy's influence**. In every situation, we must remind ourselves of our unity with Jesus. This understanding becomes a filter through which we interpret everything—our relationship with God, our authority over Satan, and our standing as believers. By seeing ourselves through the lens of Jesus' victory, we establish strong spiritual boundaries, making it much harder for the enemy's deceptions to take root. Satan's power is limited to suggestions and lies, so when we stay aligned with Christ, we are fully equipped to stand firm, free from his influence.

Reflective Questions

1. **How does understanding Satan's limitations** in our lives help us approach spiritual challenges more confidently?
2. In what ways can we actively **cast our cares upon the Lord**, ensuring that fear and worry do not become footholds for the enemy?

3. **Why is it essential to identify with Jesus** when facing temptations and suggestions from Satan?
4. How can the **story of Ananias and Sapphira** serve as a cautionary tale in our approach to truthfulness and integrity as believers?
5. What steps can we take daily to **actively protect our peace** and resist the distractions and anxieties of the world?

ACTIONABLE STEPS

- **Cultivate**: Reflect on and reinforce your understanding of your identity in Christ, reminding yourself of your authority and position as a believer. Commit to spending daily time in the Word, allowing it to reinforce your confidence in God's protection and peace.
- **Equip**: Equip yourself with Scripture that speaks about the peace and power available to believers. Memorize and internalize these verses, using them as tools to counteract any thoughts, anxieties, or suggestions that do not align with the truth of God's Word.
- **Engage**: Engage with God in prayer, intentionally casting all your cares upon Him. Trust that God will carry your burdens, freeing you to focus on His peace rather than worldly concerns.

SATAN ISN'T TRESPASSING ON YOUR BODY

JOURNALING Prompt

Reflect on any areas of your life where you have allowed fear, worry, or stress to take root. Write down these specific areas, then pray over each one, surrendering them to God. Afterward, write down any Scriptures that speak to you about God's peace and promise to protect and care for you, using these as daily affirmations of faith.

NEVER BE SICK AGAIN OFFICIAL WORKBOOK

SATAN ISN'T TRESPASSING ON YOUR BODY

CHAPTER 21
WHATEVER HAS YOUR IMAGINATION HAS YOUR FAITH

God has given us the powerful gift of imagination, not to burden us but to equip us with a tool for envisioning His promises. Our imagination serves as the canvas for our faith, drawing our focus toward the life, healing, and peace that Jesus has already secured for us. We are called to meditate on the truth of our union with Christ, envisioning His life and strength flowing through us, enabling us to remain steadfast in the reality of Heaven. When we see ourselves as God sees us, whole and free, our faith is anchored in His truth rather than our fears. Let us guard this precious tool, using it to stay connected to God's promises and His perspective on our lives.

3 John 2 NKJV: Beloved, I pray that you may prosper in all things and be in health, just as your soul prospers.

WHATEVER HAS YOUR IMAGINATION HAS YOUR FAITH

Throughout the last twenty years, the Holy Spirit has guided me down various roads of my study of divine health. It's actually fascinating as I look back and see how He has built these things in me. Outside of the foundational piece of our union with Christ, this area I want to talk to you about has been the most life-changing and inspiring piece I have come across—and hardly anyone is talking about it: our imagination. Several years ago, I was led by the Lord to go back and begin studying the subject of spirit, soul, and body. As I did so, I began to quickly see the connection of **our soul and body**. When I refer to the soul, I am referring to our mind and emotions. A lot of Christians talk about winning souls, but in reality, they mean winning spirits. We are spirit beings. It is us as spirits who are born again, but our soul/mind must be renewed. Our body is simply a follower to whatever our mind is on. I had been taught this subject when I was in Bible school many years ago, but as I began to look at it from a fresh perspective, I began to see how involved our soul is to the health we experience in our body. Notice that 3 John 2 shows there is a direct correlation between your mind and your body. You could say that **where your mind goes, your body goes**.

Now we have already established that **satan cannot make you sin** and thus cannot make you sick. He is the tempter and deceiver, and his only weapon is to bring thoughts, ideas, and suggestions with the hope that you will grab hold of them in your imagination. This is how he gets you to sin, and this is also how he gets you to get sick. Again, Eve was righteous, so satan couldn't do anything to her. All he could do was bring thoughts, ideas, and suggestions with the hope of changing her **imagination**. As he began to give Eve things to think about, instead of casting those thoughts down, she began to meditate on them. As she meditated, it changed her perspective on the tree. Your imaginations will eventually lead to manifestations. Notice in Genesis

3:6, it says, "when the woman saw." This was not the first time Eve saw the tree physically; this was the first time she saw it with deceived eyes in her imagination. Satan couldn't make her sin or make her sick. If he wanted her out of the way, how come satan did not just kill her? Why didn't satan put cancer on her? Why didn't satan grab the fruit, put it in her hand, and force her to take a bite? Because **satan couldn't just trespass and do what he wanted** to a righteous person. His only weapon was a thought.

If our weapons are not carnal but spiritual and they are for the purpose of casting down imaginations, then what type of weapon do you think satan has? What do you think satan's main endeavor is? Where do you think the real battlefield lies? **It is a battle for your imagination.** Friend, listen to me very closely: **whatever has your imagination has your faith.** For years we have thought that as Christians, we had faith problems. We have focused on steps, keys, A-B-Cs, and 1-2-3s to get more faith, but it is not a faith problem; **we have an imagination problem.** Whatever you think on the most will become your reality. You see, as righteous people in union with Christ, we have the faith of God. Faith is actually one of the fruits of the born-again spirit! Jesus gave us the tools that we need to get the job done. After all, if mustard-seed faith will move a mountain (Matthew 17:20), it must take a microscopic amount of faith to move a tumor! Most Christians are not aware of what they have; thus, they are easily deceived in their imaginations. This was the case with Eve; she was deceived (2 Corinthians 11:3) because she didn't know her identity. **Satan's deception was, "If you eat of the tree, it will make you like God."** It was the great deception because she was already like God, but she didn't know it. As a result, she began to work to get what she already was and lost what she already had.

Let me ask you this question: Is it possible that we as righteous people, the body of Christ, are in the very same position as

Eve? Is it possible that satan is telling us, "If you do this, you will get healed," despite the heavenly fact that **we are already healed?** Satan wants you always working for what you already have. Remember, if satan is telling you something, it's a lie. He is the father of lies, and there is no truth in him (John 8:44). Is it possible that satan is telling you that you aren't healed because he knows you really are? Is it possible that the reason righteous people are getting sick is because satan is telling you it is possible? He can't just do anything to your body; **he needs you to change your imagination and see it as possible** and then begin to care. When you do, whether you realize it or not, **your faith just latched onto it** and is now working to produce it. Why? Faith is the evidence of things hoped for.

Our imagination can be used for good and for bad. This is why **meditating on God's realities rather than worldly fears** is key to experiencing the fullness of life that Christ offers. Colossians reminds us to set our minds on things above, not on earthly matters. Worldly concerns may try to crowd into our thoughts, but by meditating on the truth that we are whole, righteous, and protected in Christ, we align ourselves with Heaven's perspective. As we do, God's peace flows through us, preventing the destructive effects of worry and stress. **Guarding your imagination is guarding your health.** In the Spirit-filled churches, for decades now, there has been a tremendous focus on our words and the power they carry. Friend, let me tell you right now, there is power in our words and what we speak will produce life or death. However, when it came to the teaching on our confessions, **we missed the mark.** Jesus does mention the importance of our words, but words are not the focus; the focus is on our imaginations. **The imagination is the root of our words and actions.**

Our soul is the valve that determines what flows not only into our bodies but also into our lives. **We are now holding** the power cord and determining whether we stay plugged into life or plugged into death, and what we do with our imaginations determines the flow. I am a spirit, filled with the life of God, but no life will flow in my body if my soul is connected to the things of the world. Whatever has my imagination has my faith, and **whatever has my faith will be produced in my life.** Satan has no problem with you focusing on byproducts like positive confession if you aren't working on your imagination. **The imagination is where victory or defeat is decided.**

REFLECTIVE QUESTIONS

1. How has your imagination influenced your health and well-being in the past?
2. Why do you think satan focuses on influencing your imagination rather than forcing you to sin?
3. In what ways have you allowed fear or doubt to take hold in your imagination, affecting your faith?
4. How can meditating on God's promises shift the way you view challenges in your life?
5. What steps can you take to ensure your imagination aligns with God's truths?

ACTIONABLE STEPS

- **Cultivate**: Begin each day by intentionally filling your imagination with images of God's promises. Imagine yourself walking in health, peace, and purpose as you connect with His Word.

- **Equip**: Memorize and meditate on scriptures that affirm your identity in Christ. Let these scriptures guide your thoughts, especially when challenges arise.
- **Engage**: Practice using your imagination to see God's reality in your life. Take a few moments each day to envision your life through the lens of His promises.

Journaling Prompt

Reflect on an area of your life where you've allowed fear to capture your imagination. How would that situation look if you aligned your imagination with God's promises instead? Write down specific ways you can shift your perspective to embrace His truth fully.

WHATEVER HAS YOUR IMAGINATION HAS YOUR FAITH

CHAPTER 22
STAY CONNECTED TO THE SOURCE

Remain in the place of divine grace where your efforts are minimized and His power is maximized. God has already provided all you need through Christ; your part is simply to abide in this truth.

"But seek first the kingdom of God and His righteousness, and all these things shall be added to you." - Matthew 6:33 NKJV

As we explore the depths of our faith and the intricacies of our spiritual walk, it becomes clear that **dependence on Christ's provision** is foundational. In our journey with Christ, we learn that grace, not our personal efforts, provides everything we need for healing and spiritual growth. Grace has placed within us everything necessary for our well-being, and recognizing this can transform how we live out our faith. This understanding shifts our focus from striving to achieve to simply receiving what has already been freely given.

In connection to this, our **union with Christ** is pivotal. Like branches on a vine, our spiritual life flows directly from our connection to Him. This union is not just a theological concept but a living, breathing relationship that sustains us. As we maintain our connection with Christ, we find that fruitfulness naturally follows. This fruitfulness is a direct result of our ongoing and intimate relationship with Him, highlighting why it is so essential to remain closely knit to our Source.

However, many of us fall into the trap of self-reliance, especially in spiritual matters. The **dangers of self-effort in spiritual matters** become apparent when we tirelessly attempt to secure our healing or spiritual progress through actions like frequent confessions, extensive scripture reading, or a flurry of religious activities. While these practices are important for growth and maintaining our fellowship with God, they are not the mechanisms by which we receive what grace has already provided. This distinction is crucial for preventing frustration and spiritual fatigue.

This leads us to the crucial aspect of **understanding true faith**. True faith is more than just an acknowledgment of doctrines; it arises from hearing the voice of God—a Rhema word—through which God speaks directly into our situations. This form of communication with God goes beyond the mere reading of scripture to engaging with the Holy Spirit who brings the written word to life in our hearts.

Engaging in **praying in the Spirit** is another transformative practice. This form of prayer enhances our consciousness of God's presence and aligns our desires with His. As we pray in the Spirit, we are not only speaking to God but also listening, creating a dynamic interaction where we co-labor with God in the spiritual realm. This form of prayer is essential for maintaining our spiritual vitality and ensuring that we are continually filled with His power and guidance.

The role of spiritual encounters in our walk with God cannot be overstated. These are not one-time experiences but should be a regular part of our spiritual life. Each encounter with God is designed to transform us, increasing our awareness of His presence and aligning us more closely with His purposes. These moments remind us of Moses, who radiated God's glory after spending time in His presence, or Jesus, whose life was a testament to living in continuous communion with the Father.

Moreover, it is vital to understand the importance of **fellowship vs. performance**. Our relationship with God should not be measured by how much we 'do' in terms of spiritual activities but by the quality of our fellowship with Him. It is in the place of fellowship where we truly grow and where the power of God is most evident in our lives.

Awareness of God's presence is a barometer of our spiritual condition. A decrease in this awareness can lead us to a state of spiritual backsliding, where we become less attuned to the divine and more susceptible to the mundane and material distractions of life. Staying aware of God's immediate presence keeps our spiritual life vibrant and active.

Focusing on **the impact of divine focus** can radically alter our experience of life's challenges. By maintaining our focus on God rather than our problems, we can live from a position of victory and authority. Like Jesus, who rarely spoke of the illnesses He healed but rather the kingdom He proclaimed, we too can learn to see beyond the temporal to the eternal realities of God's kingdom.

Lastly, adopting a **lifestyle of spiritual discipline**—regularly engaging in scripture study, prayer, and moments of solitude with God—ensures that our spiritual roots go deep. This disciplined approach to our spiritual life is not about rigidity but about maintaining an open channel through which God's life can flow into and through us.

By embracing these principles, we align ourselves more closely with God's intentions for us, experiencing a life marked not only by divine health but by a profound impact on the world around us.

REFLECTIVE QUESTIONS

1. What are some areas of your life where you might be relying more on your efforts than on God's grace?
2. How can you cultivate a deeper awareness of your union with Christ daily?
3. In what ways have you confused acquiring biblical knowledge with developing a true relationship with God?
4. Can you identify times when praying in the Spirit significantly impacted your spiritual life? What were the outcomes?
5. How can regular encounters with God change your perspective on the challenges you face?

ACTIONABLE STEPS

- **Cultivate an environment of continual fellowship**: Set aside daily times for reading the Word with the intent to listen to what God is saying specifically to you. Create a dedicated space in your home where you can be free from distractions to engage with God.

- **Equip yourself with knowledge of the Spirit's voice**: Regularly practice distinguishing the voice of the Holy Spirit from your thoughts through journaling insights and confirmations from your prayer time and scripture study.
- **Engage in consistent spiritual disciplines**: Commit to a routine that balances scripture study, prayer, and meditative silence. This routine should aim to deepen your connection with God and equip you to handle spiritual and daily challenges more effectively.

Journaling **Prompt**

Reflect on your current spiritual practices. Are they leading you into deeper fellowship with God, or are they merely religious activities? How can you transform these practices to become more about communion with God rather than performance?

STAY CONNECTED TO THE SOURCE

CHAPTER 23
WHEN CHRISTIANS ARE SICK

Stand firm in the victory over sin and sickness that Christ has already won for you. Live from a place of health and wholeness, knowing that your faith has made you well.

"But He was wounded for our transgressions, He was bruised for our iniquities; The chastisement for our peace was upon Him, And by His stripes we are healed." - Isaiah 53:5 NKJV

In this chapter, we confront a significant paradox within the Christian life: how can we, who are declared dead to sin and its consequences through Christ, still find ourselves battling sickness? This dilemma calls for a profound shift in our **mindset towards sickness**. It's crucial to understand that just as we are dead to sin, we can view ourselves as dead to sickness as well. The notion that sickness can still dominate our lives persists only because we allow it space in our minds and lives. If we truly believe, as scripture tells us, that we are free from sin's grasp, then this freedom extends to all sin's byproducts, including sickness.

Central to our ability to stand firm in health is our **imagination**. What we visualize regularly can manifest in our lives. If we persist in imagining sickness as a probable part of our lives, it becomes a self-fulfilling prophecy. Conversely, envisioning ourselves as vibrant and full of life can have a protective and healing effect. This power of visualization isn't just about positive thinking; it's about aligning our thoughts with God's truth about our lives.

Moreover, the state of our physical health is deeply intertwined with our spiritual condition, emphasizing the **spiritual and physical health connection**. Our body is a temple of the Holy Spirit, and neglecting this temple can lead to physical ailments. Just as we are called to be stewards of our spiritual gifts, we are also tasked with the care of our physical bodies. This stewardship is not about vanity or fear but about respecting the divine presence within us.

The act of communion is another profound point of reflection. In taking communion, we are not merely performing a ritual; we are partaking in the profound spiritual process of affirming our **power of communion** with Christ's death and resurrection. Misunderstanding or approaching this sacrament superficially can lead to a disconnection between our declared faith and our lived experience. Each time we partake in communion, we must remember that it symbolizes our death to sin and life in Christ, which includes victory over sickness.

Condemnation often creeps into our thoughts, especially when we face health challenges. This condemnation can make us feel unworthy or spiritually insufficient, which can manifest in physical symptoms. We must reject these voices of condemnation and cling to the truth that in Christ, we are whole and healed.

A proactive stance in our health involves making **declarations of health**. By speaking life and health over our bodies, we align ourselves with God's word. These declarations help fortify our faith and shield us from accepting illness as an inevitable plight.

Our environment and culture also play significant roles in shaping our health perceptions. The constant barrage of pharmaceutical advertisements and a societal focus on disease prevention can lead us away from biblical health principles. Recognizing and resisting this **cultural influence on health** is crucial if we are to maintain a biblically grounded perspective on our health.

In cases where sickness has overtaken us, the Bible provides a protocol involving the church community. **Elders' role in healing** is to stand with us in prayer, reinforcing the collective faith of the community in God's healing power. This is a testament to the strength and necessity of communal support in our walk with Christ.

Living in continuous **life in the Spirit** protects us from physical and spiritual harm. The Holy Spirit's guidance is crucial not just for avoiding spiritual pitfalls but also for navigating our daily lives safely, free from accidents and harmful incidents.

Lastly, overcoming the **fear of death** is essential for living a life of divine health. This fear is often the root of many health anxieties and can keep us in bondage. Recognizing that death has no hold on us through Christ liberates us to live fully, unafraid of the physical cessation of life.

By embracing these principles and living out the truths of our faith, we can navigate our Christian journey not just with spiritual vitality but also with robust physical health. This holistic approach to living is not just about personal well-being but about bearing witness to the transformative power of Christ's death and resurrection in every aspect of our lives.

Reflective Questions

1. How has your belief in the possibility of sickness impacted your health?
2. In what ways can you cultivate a healthier imagination regarding your physical and spiritual life?
3. How well do you care for your physical body as the temple of the Holy Spirit?
4. How does partaking in communion shape your understanding of health?
5. What fears related to health do you need to overcome to walk in divine health?

Actionable Steps

- **Cultivate a Godly Imagination**: Regularly visualize your life free from sickness, meditating on scriptures that affirm your health in Christ. This practice will align your spiritual and physical realities.
- **Equip Yourself with Knowledge of the Spirit's Guidance**: Actively seek the Holy Spirit's guidance in daily decisions to avoid physical dangers and ailments. This can include asking for insight during prayer or while reading the Bible.
- **Engage in Health Declarations**: Daily declare your freedom from sickness and your entitlement to divine

health. These declarations reinforce your spiritual beliefs and can manifest in your physical health.

Journaling **Prompt**

Reflect on the last time you felt physically unwell and consider the thoughts or beliefs you held about your health at that time. How can aligning your thoughts with God's truth about health change your approach to dealing with sickness in the future?

NEVER BE SICK AGAIN OFFICIAL WORKBOOK

WHEN CHRISTIANS ARE SICK

CHAPTER 24
ACCIDENTS AND INJURIES

Embrace the fullness of God's promise to protect and guide you through the Holy Spirit. As you deepen your relationship with Him and heed His guidance, you can navigate life with an assurance of safety and divine oversight.

"He shall give His angels charge over you, to keep you in all your ways. In their hands they shall bear you up, Lest you dash your foot against a stone." - Psalm 91:11-12 NKJV

In this chapter, we explore a profound truth revealed through scripture and personal experiences—the protective oversight provided by the Holy Spirit. The belief that **Holy Spirit's Guidance Prevents Accidents** is not merely a theological concept but a practical aspect of our daily lives. Emphasizing this point is essential because it reflects the fact that, according to scripture, every incident or injury among Christians is due to not heeding the Holy Spirit's direction. This is a strong statement, yet it is grounded in the truth that scriptural wisdom provides a foundation for divine protection.

Psalm 91's Promise of Protection offers us an incredible assurance from God—that those who fully trust in Him are shielded from harm. This scripture is not a poetic overstatement but a literal promise of safety that extends to the prevention of physical injuries. The passage assures us that no evil will conquer those who make God their refuge, illustrating a life untouched by physical harm, to the point of not even stubbing a toe.

Moreover, this divine protection involves the **Role of Angels in Physical Safety**. Scripture states that angels are commissioned to protect us, preventing even minor injuries like stubbing a toe. This key point highlights that our protection is not passive but involves active intervention from heavenly beings, ensuring that even the smallest potential harm is avoided.

The **Holy Spirit as Our Guide** serves a pivotal role in our daily decisions and movements. Described as a tour guide who has already traversed our path, the Holy Spirit knows the potential pitfalls and dangers ahead. By following His lead, we can navigate through life not only safe from spiritual falls but also from physical accidents.

Despite these divine provisions, ignoring the Holy Spirit's promptings can lead to unnecessary hardships, as detailed in the key point about the **Consequences of Ignoring Spiritual Guidance**. Personal anecdotes from believers, including my own, serve as stark reminders that our spiritual attentiveness can have real-world implications, affecting our physical well-being and financial stability.

The **Immediate and Long-Term Impacts of Accidents** are not to be overlooked. Injuries can result in prolonged physical pain or permanent disability, further emphasizing why adhering to spiritual guidance is crucial not only for our spiritual health but also for our physical longevity.

However, our faith also teaches us about recovery and restoration, as seen in the **Healing and Divine Intervention Post-Accident**. The miraculous healings that many have experienced post-accident underscore that even when we fail to listen, God's grace and the life-giving power within us can restore and heal.

It's also crucial to adopt a proactive approach to this divine guidance, as outlined in the **Importance of Being Proactive in Spiritual Listening**. Daily life requires us to be vigilant and responsive to the Holy Spirit's subtle cues, which can safeguard us against both major catastrophes and minor accidents.

The **Intersection of Spiritual Authority and Physical Reality** demonstrates that our spiritual beliefs have tangible effects on our physical circumstances. By exercising spiritual authority through faith and obedience, we can influence our physical environment to align with God's protective promises.

Lastly, understanding and believing in these principles provide us with **Empowerment Through Knowledge and Faith**. This empowerment is crucial for living a life that transcends mere survival, allowing us to thrive in both spiritual and physical realms by walking confidently in God's promises of protection and well-being.

By embracing and applying these principles, we live not in fear of what might come but in the assurance of God's comprehensive protection. This chapter aims not only to inform but to transform how we view and interact with our world, encouraging a life of faith that actively engages with divine promises for our safety and health.

ACCIDENTS AND INJURIES

REFLECTIVE QUESTIONS

1. How has understanding the Holy Spirit's role as a guide changed your perspective on daily decision-making?
2. Can you recall a situation where you felt a clear directive from the Holy Spirit that you either followed or ignored? What was the outcome?
3. In what ways can you increase your sensitivity to the Holy Spirit's guidance to prevent potential accidents?
4. How do you reconcile the promise of Psalm 91 with experiences of believers who have suffered harm?
5. What steps can you take to more actively engage with God's protective promises in your daily life?

ACTIONABLE STEPS

- **Cultivate Daily Sensitivity to the Holy Spirit**: Begin each day with a prayer for sensitivity and guidance, asking the Holy Spirit to alert you to any dangers and guide your steps throughout the day.
- **Equip Yourself with Scriptural Promises of Protection**: Regularly study and memorize scriptures like Psalm 91 that emphasize God's protection. Keeping these promises at the forefront of your mind will strengthen your faith in God's protective power.
- **Engage in Regular Spiritual Check-Ins**: Set aside time each day to reflect on and journal about how you are experiencing the Holy Spirit's guidance. Note any promptings you feel and the actions you took in

response, assessing how these decisions impacted your safety and well-being.

JOURNALING Prompt

Reflect on the ways you currently respond to the Holy Spirit's guidance. Consider times when you've felt a prompting and either followed or ignored it. How can you improve your responsiveness to ensure your safety and well-being in line with God's promises?

ACCIDENTS AND INJURIES

NEVER BE SICK AGAIN OFFICIAL WORKBOOK

CHAPTER 25
FOOD AND DRUGS

Trust in the Lord and His provisions for health and wellness. God has equipped us with all we need for a life of health and vitality, reflected in the food He provides and the bodies He has

> "Or do you not know that your body is the temple of the Holy Spirit who is in you, whom you have from God, and you are not your own?" 1 Corinthians 6:19 NKJV

Writing to you about the critical issue of **Your Body, God's Temple**, it becomes clear that understanding our bodies as the dwelling place of the Holy Spirit is foundational. This isn't just a metaphorical expression; it's a practical reality that should guide our daily health choices. Recognizing that **you are not your own** prompts a deeper respect and care for the physical vessel God has entrusted to us. This perspective changes how we view everything from the food we eat to the activities we engage in.

As we continue, it's impossible to overlook the **Direct Cause and Effect** relationship between our lifestyle choices and our health. Many of today's prevalent diseases, such as diabetes and heart disease, are exacerbated by our dietary choices—particularly our consumption of processed foods. These conditions are not just unfortunate inevitabilities but are often **self-inflicted** through poor dietary habits. This reality isn't meant to assign blame but to empower us with the knowledge to make changes.

One cannot help but consider what God initially provided for sustenance. In the covenant with Noah, God outlined a diet that included all things that moved and the green herbs—**Balance in Diet** was inherent in these instructions. This divine guideline highlights the variety and balance necessary for a healthy diet, emphasizing that both animal and plant-based foods have their place on our tables.

The issue of **Dangers of Processed Foods** is particularly troubling. Our shift from natural foods to those that are industrially manufactured—**Ultra-processed foods**—has led to a significant increase in lifestyle-related diseases. These foods, while convenient, are laden with additives that our bodies are not designed to process effectively.

Moreover, the widespread use of **High-Fructose Corn Syrup** in the American diet exemplifies the harmful economic trade-offs made at the expense of public health. This artificial sweetener is not just another ingredient; it's a major contributor to the obesity epidemic and other metabolic diseases that plague our society.

Addressing the economic motivations behind food production leads us to the sad truth that many decisions in the food industry are made with profit in mind, not the well-being of the consumer. This **Economic vs. Nutritional Value** dilemma means that cheaper, more addictive, and nutritionally void food options are ubiquitously available, which misguides many on their eating habits.

Confronting these truths, it becomes evident that proactive

steps are required to safeguard our health. **Physical Activity's Role** in maintaining health cannot be overstated. By integrating regular physical activities into our routine, we not only enhance our metabolic efficiency but also improve our overall well-being, from mental clarity to physical stamina.

In terms of treatment, the reliance on medications to manage symptoms highlights a profound disconnect in our approach to health. **Medication and Healing** should not be about merely managing diseases but fostering an environment within our bodies where true healing can occur. Medications often do not address the underlying causes of disease—they manage the symptoms, which prolongs the illness.

Finally, the realization of **Personal Responsibility** in managing our health is key. We must take active steps to control what we eat, how we move, and the way we treat our bodies. This isn't just about avoiding illness but about thriving in the full health that God intends for us.

Reflecting on these points offers a comprehensive view of how intertwined our spiritual beliefs and physical practices should be. It's not just about healing from diseases but preventing them by making informed, God-honoring choices every day. This holistic approach to health not only honors God but also enhances our quality of life, allowing us to serve Him better in all aspects of our lives.

REFLECTIVE QUESTIONS

1. How does recognizing your body as a temple influence your daily health choices?
2. In what ways can you reduce your intake of processed foods to improve your health?

3. How does the balance of nutrients in your current diet compare with the dietary advice given to Noah and his family?
4. Reflect on a time when a simple change in diet or exercise made a significant difference in your health. What did you learn from that experience?
5. How can understanding the economic motivations behind food production influence your food choices?

ACTIONABLE STEPS

Cultivate a Balanced Diet: Begin by reviewing your current eating habits and make a conscious effort to introduce more natural, unprocessed foods into your diet each week.

Equip Yourself with Knowledge: Educate yourself about the nutritional content of your food. Start reading labels more critically to avoid high-fructose corn syrup and excessive additives.

Engage in Regular Physical Activity: Set a manageable goal to increase your physical activity. Start with something as simple as a daily walk, gradually increasing intensity and variety.

JOURNALING **Prompt**

Reflect on your current health practices: What are you doing well? Where could you improve? How can you start making changes that align your lifestyle more closely with the biblical view of your body as a temple?

FOOD AND DRUGS

Harrison House is a Spirit-filled, Word of Faith Christian publisher dedicated to spreading the message of faith, hope, and love through our wide range of inspiring publications. Committed to the messages that highlight the power of the Word and Spirit, we provide books, devotionals, and study guides that empower believers to live victorious, faith-filled lives.

Our resources are designed to help readers grow spiritually, strengthen their faith, and experience the transformative power of God's Word. Harrison House is passionate about equipping Christians with the tools they need to fulfill their divine purpose and impact the world for Christ.

www.ingramcontent.com/pod-product-compliance
Lightning Source LLC
Chambersburg PA
CBHW062106080426
42734CB00012B/2770